PRAISE FOR
LEAD with H.O.P.E.

LEAD WITH H.O.P.E. is a deeply moving guide that blends personal resilience, educational leadership, and evidence-based strategies into a framework every educator and leader can embrace. Dr. Brandi Kelly's vulnerability, insight, and practical tools illuminate how trauma can be transformed into triumph through the H.O.P.E. system: Habits, Optimism, Purpose, Passion, Perseverance, and Excellence. With inspiring storytelling and actionable steps, this book is a powerful reminder that hope isn't just an emotion – it's a leadership strategy that builds self-efficacy, drives culture change, and empowers us to lead with heart and intention.

Kim Strobel
Keynote Speaker, School Leader, Happiness Coach, Strobel Education, LLC

There are plenty of books on leadership and trauma, but few live at their intersection like *Lead With H.O.P.E.* by Dr. Brandi Kelly. It's authentic, practical, and acutely personal. Dr. Kelly doesn't sugarcoat the weight of leadership. She names the fear, the doubt, and the grind – then uses those moments to teach, reflect, and grow. Her H.O.P.E. system isn't just an acronym; it's a roadmap rooted in self-efficacy. This isn't a book of quick fixes. It's an invitation to lead with purpose, integrity, and conviction. Vulnerable, honest, and timely, this book challenges leaders to build systems – and people – through hope in action. Required reading for those serious about leading from the inside out.

PJ Caposey
Superintendent of OCUSD 220, Author, Leadership Coach

I highly recommend this book! Dr. Brandi Kelly delivers what so many others miss – deliberate practice and a systemic approach. It's clear that success isn't about lofty goals; it's about building the habits, structures, and mindset to actually reach them. With honesty, heart, and decades of experience, the author thoughtfully lays out a process for self-efficacy that empowers educators and students alike. *LEAD WITH H.O.P.E.* is a timely and practical guide for anyone ready to lead with purpose and create lasting impact!

Charle Peck
Keynote Speaker, Author, School Mental Health Consultant

Dr. Brandi Kelly's *LEAD WITH H.O.P.E.* is a powerful and inspiring guide for anyone seeking to lead with purpose and resilience. Through compelling stories and practical reflection, she offers a roadmap to building a personalized system of self-efficacy rooted in HOPE. This book is more than a read, it's a transformational experience that empowers readers to believe in themselves, act with intention, and lead with heart. A must-have for every current and aspiring leader.

Tom Mahoney
Superintendent, Speaker, Coach

This inspiring book offers educators a thoughtful guide to personal and professional growth through the H.O.P.E. system. Each area – Habits, Optimistic Outlook, Purpose, Passion, Perseverance, and Excellence – invites reflection and equips educators with practical tools to build self-awareness and self-efficacy. This book is a must-read for those seeking to lead with purpose, resilience, and a renewed sense of impact in their work.

Julie Schmidt Hasson
Professor, Researcher, Resilience Trainer

Lead with Hope, by Dr. Brandi Kelly, is a must-read for educational leaders navigating the complexities of today's school environments. With a powerful blend of heart, strategy, and vision, Dr. Kelly offers more than inspiration – she provides a roadmap for leading with courage, clarity, and compassion. Grounded in real-world experience and fueled by a deep belief in the transformative power of hope, this book equips leaders to rise above challenges, cultivate resilience, and create meaningful impact in their communities.

Dr. Jill M. Siler
TASA Deputy Executive Director, Author of Thrive Through the Five: Practical Truths to Powerfully Lead in Challenging Times

In *Lead with H.O.P.E.*, Dr. Brandi Kelly offers more than just a personal story of overcoming tragedy – this is a blueprint for transforming any challenge into a moment of growth. With actionable insights and a clear system for building self-efficacy, this book is essential for anyone looking to foster resilience in themselves and their communities. It's not just about surviving – it's about thriving through the power of HOPE and consistent action.

Damon West
Best-Selling Author of The Coffee Bean

Dr. Brandi Kelly's *Lead with H.O.P.E.* is the companion every school leader needs. Rooted in Dr. Kelly's empathetic voice and human-centered insight, this book offers a heartfelt blueprint for leading with meaning and intention. In these pages, you'll find more than inspiration – you'll find practical strategies to build a culture where hope thrives. Dr. Kelly reminds us that leadership is a calling of connection and courage. This is a powerful guide for those ready to lead with heart, purpose, and a deep belief in what's possible. A true anthem for the leadership journey.

Sean Gaillard
Principal

Dr. Kelly presents a compelling framework for building self-efficacy through her H.O.P.E. system: Habits, Optimistic Outlook, Purpose/Passion/Perseverance, and Excellence. Drawing from personal experiences with trauma and her career in education, she demonstrates how this system can transform leadership and personal growth. Dr. Kelly balances research with accessible, personal storytelling to show how self-awareness and intentional practices create resilience. This practical guide provides actionable strategies, self-reflection exercises, and real-world examples for educators, leaders, and anyone seeking to overcome adversity and inspire others. Well done! An important read and an excellent demonstration of vulnerability.

Dr. Jenni Donohoo
Education Consultant and Author

I can't tell you enough how much I was moved when reading *Lead with H.O.P.E.* Brandi Kelly has truly created a must have guide for every school leader. Not only did it move my heart, but it also gave me easy, actionable items. This is the kind of book I can look forward coming back to again and again!

Todd Nesloney
International Speaker, Best Selling Author
Director of Culture and Strategic Leadership for TEPSA

LEAD
with
H.O.P.E.

Building a System of Self-Efficacy

Dr. Brandi Kelly

Lead with H.O.P.E.: Building a System of Self-Efficacy

Copyright © by Dr. Brandi Kelly
First Edition 2025

All rights reserved.

No part of this publication may be reproduced in any form, or by any means, electronic or mechanical, including photocopying, recording, or any information browsing, storage or retrieval system, without permission in writing from the publisher.

Road to Awesome, LLC.

ACKNOWLEDGEMENTS

Writing a book has always been a dream of mine. But if I'm being honest, it wasn't just my passion for words or my love of storytelling that made it possible. No, it was the unwavering support, the love, and the encouragement from the incredible people in my life – my family – that truly made this journey possible.

It all starts with Jeremy, my husband, and my best friend. There's no way I could have made it through this process without his constant belief in me. His encouragement, his patience, and his ability to ground me when the path seemed unclear were the steady pillars I leaned on. Jeremy – you are my strength, you are my rock, and I will forever be grateful for you.

Then there's my daughter, Morgan. She's been there, cheering me on every step of the way. Morgan, you are more than I could ever hope for in a daughter, and I'm so grateful for you.

Ryan, my son, has been my steady source of truth. He's the one who will always tell me like it is – whether I want to hear it or not. Ryan, your honesty has been a gift, I cherish it, and I will always cherish you.

And then there's Josiah, my son-in-law, and Brianna, my daughter-in-law. Both of you are such kind-hearted, compassionate souls. You have been the perfect partners for my children and have added so much love and strength to our growing family. Your steady presence has been a reminder that love and support go beyond just bloodlines – our family is built on a foundation of care and trust. Thank you both for being exactly who you are.

Last, my grandsons: Jensen, Rhett, and Beau. You are the lights of my life, the joy I didn't know was possible. Every hug, every smile, every giggle reminds me of the magic that exists in the world. To see the world through your eyes has been one of the greatest blessings I could have ever asked for. I love you all more than words can express, and I'm so thankful for the happiness you bring into my life every single day.

To my entire family – thank you for being my inspiration, my support, my reason for pushing forward when it seemed impossible. I love you all to the moon and back, and I'm deeply grateful for each one of you. My greatest wish is that you will always lead a life filled with hope, faith, and love!

TABLE OF CONTENTS

INTRODUCTION	1
CHAPTER ONE *Creating a System for Improving Self-Efficacy*	5
CHAPTER TWO *H is for Habits*	17
CHAPTER THREE *O is for Optimistic Outlook*	31
CHAPTER FOUR *P is for Purpose, Passion, and Perseverance*	49
CHAPTER FIVE *E is for Excellence*	59
CHAPTER SIX *Creating an Action Plan*	71
CHAPTER SEVEN *Building a Culture of H.O.P.E.*	87
CONCLUSION	97
REFERENCES	101
ABOUT THE AUTHOR	103

INTRODUCTION

"A leader is a dealer in hope."
~Napoleon Bonaparte

If you are reading this, it is safe to assume you are a leader – whether in the classroom, the boardroom, or in the lives of those around you. And if you are like many of us, you are searching for hope. Hope is more than just a passing wish or fleeting optimism; it is a tangible force driving us forward when things seem uncertain. Hope is a science. It is a cognitive practice, a skill that can be nurtured and developed. Hope involves setting clear goals and working toward them with clarity and intention. And leaders are dealers in hope.

Throughout our lives, we encounter innumerable moments where hope sustains us. It helps us navigate the darkness, offering the belief that something better is on the horizon. For educators – those tasked with empowering, inspiring, and educating our children – hope is not just a need but a necessity. It is the fuel that keeps us going, even on the hardest days.

For me, the journey toward hope began at 15 when I experienced a trauma that would change the trajectory of my life. It was in that moment of crisis I discovered my calling to education. My desire to give back and help others overcome their hardships allowed me to overcome the hardships that had shaped my story. I came to understand something profound: trauma doesn't have to lead to tragedy. It can be the spark that ignites our greatest success.

In the following years, I developed the H.O.P.E. system, a deliberate practice designed to help individuals tap into their inner strength and resilience. The principles of Habits, Optimistic Outlook, Purpose, Passion, Perseverance, and Excellence have become my guiding light and have enabled me to inspire others to do the same.

In this book, I want to share with you the tools and practices that have helped me, and countless others, ignite hope within ourselves and our communities. Because no matter where you are or what challenges you face, hope is always within reach. And together, we can harness its power to create meaningful change. **Let's spark H.O.P.E. together!**

LEAD with H.O.P.E.

HABITS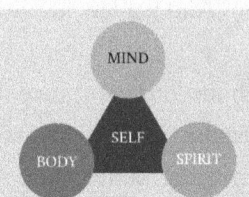

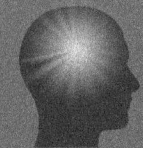 **OPTIMISTIC OUTLOOK**

PURPOSE
PASSION
PERSEVERANCE

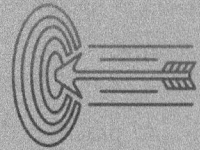 **EXCELLENCE**

sparkhopeedu.com

CHAPTER ONE
Creating a System for Improving Self-Efficacy

"You do not rise to the level of your goals. You fall to the level of your systems."
~*James Clear*

"You don't rise to the level of your goals; you fall to the level of your systems." This quote by James Clear resonates deeply with me and helped me develop my system of H.O.P.E. Through a focus on systems thinking, I began to recognize the importance of intentional, structured processes in achieving long-term success.

I have been in education for over 20 years, beginning my career in 2001 as a School Social Work Intern in Effingham School District. I have special memories from my time there where I had a wonderful mentor, Kim Varner, and collaborated with a team of dedicated educators. Together, we worked hard to ensure students received the best education possible. While Effingham had strong programs in place, I truly believe it's the people, not the programs, that make education great. This truth remains at the heart of education, both in the past and moving forward.

I spent over a decade at Effingham before transitioning into Educational Administration. When I decided to go into administration, I remember a student's mother asking me why I would go to the "dark side." My short answer was I wanted to be a change agent, and I believed this was the next right thing for me in my career. As you will see, I had a lot to learn.

I spent 10 years as a principal in three different schools, with my first role being at Ramsey Grade School. Located in a high-poverty area with over 60% of students from low-income families, my time at Ramsey was among the most rewarding of my career. I have always felt passionate about serving at-risk students, a purpose inspired during my time as a student at Ramsey High School.

While I attended Ramsey, my family and I endured a tragedy that shaped my life in profound ways. During that difficult time, the support my family and I received from the community left a lasting impact on me. This experience instilled a deep sense of gratitude in me and motivated me to give back to a community that had shown so much care and compassion. That sense of purpose has guided me throughout my career. At Ramsey, I understood firsthand the importance of providing a supportive, caring environment during challenging times. This commitment to service and community continues to shape my vision for the future of education.

Once my children had graduated from Ramsey High School, I received the opportunity to serve as the Principal at McGaughey Elementary School. This was an exciting opportunity because it offered me the possibility to grow as an educational leader. I had no idea what I was signing up for when my husband and I moved to Mt. Zion. The student population was around 20% low income, and each day brought a new opportunity. With almost 400 students ranging from ages three to seven, every day was all hands on deck. The physical energy it took to lead a building with the many needs of our little learners left me exhausted. I have come to appreciate the gifts and talents of our early childhood educators. These men and women are truly special people.

During my time at McGaughey, I learned a lot about climate and culture, which shaped me as a leader. These lessons deepened my understanding of how crucial it is to create an environment where both students and staff feel valued, supported, and empowered. I came to realize that a positive school climate isn't just about maintaining order – it's about nurturing relationships, building trust, and fostering a sense of belonging. As a leader, I learned that a strong, positive culture directly influences student achievement and staff morale, and it is essential to consistently model and reinforce the values that define that culture. These experiences have informed my leadership practice, particularly in how I approach decision-making and support others in their growth.

Due to a desire to work with older students again, in 2020, I accepted a position at Sangamon Valley Middle School (SVMS). My time at SVMS was amidst the pandemic. Despite the turbulent times and a great deal of stress, we collaboratively rewrote our vision and mission statements, implemented Professional Learning Communities (PLCs), and implemented best practices around student learning, virtual learning, and Response to Intervention (RtI). I am in awe of the caring, compassionate educators I had the pleasure to work with at SVMS. Collaboratively, we helped our students deal with trauma, abuse, neglect, grief, and much, much more as we endeavored to help them learn and grow into better humans. These educators understood that educating the whole child was essential. The needs were immense, but I loved going to work every day, motivating and inspiring others to reach their full potential.

My next role in education was superintendent at Mt. Olive Community Unit School District #5. I noticed a lot of similarities in Mt. Olive to my hometown of Ramsey, IL, which is probably what drew me to this position. The most notable similarities between the two districts were they both serve PreK-12 grade students under one roof and they are both in rural central Illinois. Each district is home to caring educators and small class sizes, fostering a close-knit, supportive learning environment. During my time at Mt. Olive, we collectively worked toward the goal of improving culture and climate, implementing systems, processes and procedures to support students and grow leaders. The work was hard, but it was truly a labor of love.

Over the years, I have changed and evolved as an educator and a leader. While I am still learning and growing, I have used my H.O.P.E. system of self-efficacy to help me navigate the traumas I've faced in life and to become the educator and leader I am today. This system has provided me with the resilience, clarity, and intention needed to face challenges head-on and continue to grow, both personally and professionally.

HOPE DEFINED

To explain my sense of hope for the future, I will start with a working definition. The Oxford dictionary defines hope as: 1. A feeling of expectation and desire for a certain thing to happen; and 2. A feeling of trust.

Imagine a time when you were filled with expectation or desire for something to happen. We have all had that feeling: on Christmas morning, awaiting the birth of our child, looking forward to the return of a family member from active duty. There are an inordinate number of times throughout our life when we experience the feeling of hope. What a wonderful feeling it is! Conversely, when hope is deferred or delayed, the heart becomes sick. Heart sickness can be experienced in a number of ways such as feeling sad, discouraged, having heightened anxiety, or even depression. This emotional distress can manifest as sadness, anxiety, or even depression. A report from US News and World Report indicates that one in ten Americans experience depression (Howard, 2023). From 2015 to 2020, depression rose fastest among teens and young adults ages 12 and older. The need for hope and the systems that support self-efficacy to nurture high hope, is more important than ever.

This growing emotional distress highlights the importance of cultivating hope, which is where the concept of self-efficacy comes into play, providing a base for sustaining hope even in challenging times. Rick Snyder was a psychologist best known for his work on hope theory. He developed a framework for understanding hope and its role in personal well-being, motivation, and goal achievement. Snyder explains that self-efficacy is about believing you can do certain tasks or actions, while hope is about believing you can reach your goals. Hope consists of goals, agency, and pathways.

According to Snyder's Hope Theory , hope requires willpower and waypower. "Hope is the sum of the mental willpower and waypower you have for your goals" (Snyder, 1994). Willpower is the mental aptitude for achieving goals. Waypower is the mental map or the plan you have for achieving your goals. Both willpower and waypower are necessary to produce high hope environments. A system of self-efficacy creates willpower and waypower; in turn, producing a high hope environment.

Hope is one of the greatest predictors of academic and life success. The good news is, we can measure it with Dr. Rick Snyder's Hope Survey, a psychological assessment designed to measure an individual's levels of hope, which is defined as the ability to set goals, develop strategies to achieve them, and maintain the motivation to pursue those goals. Based on Snyder's Hope Theory, the survey breaks hope into two key components: agency or willpower – the motivation to move toward goals and pathways and waypower – the planning to achieve those goals (Snyder, 1994).

The Hope Survey can be taken by individuals in various settings—students, educators, employees, or anyone seeking to assess and improve their levels of hope. Typically, the survey is taken every six months to a year to assess changes in hope and track progress in goal-setting and motivation. However, the frequency can vary based on personal goals or the specific context in which it is used. Regular reflection on hope can be invaluable for tracking personal growth and refining strategies for success. Research consistently shows that overall well-being and success are strongly linked to high levels of hope.

When we look at the impact of hope on student outcomes, the difference is clear: Compared to schools with low-hope scores, high-hope scoring schools have a 73% higher rate of students achieving the satisfactory requirement for post-secondary readiness in all subjects (Gallup, 2019). As I said before, hope is a dependent variable. It is reliant on action to create results. The time is now to create high-hope environments, particularly in our schools. Keep in mind, what we focus on grows. It's time to change the conversation, move away from what is wrong and start focusing on what is right. It's time to take ACTION!

CULTIVATING SELF-EFFICACY AND LEADERSHIP

In May 2023, I graduated from Saint Louis University (SLU) with my doctoral degree in Educational Leadership. During my time at SLU, I studied self-efficacy, leader efficacy, and collective teacher efficacy. My project team wrote a dissertation entitled *Perceptions of School Leaders on Establishing and Sustaining Systems to Foster Collective Teacher Efficacy (Draper, Kelly, Molina, 2023)*. This project provided me with additional evidence to support the need for a system of H.O.P.E. and building self-efficacy.

According to Albert Bandura (1977), self-efficacy is "the conviction that one can successfully execute the behavior required to produce outcomes." Without self-efficacy, there can be no collective teacher efficacy. Developing self-efficacy relies on four sources: mastery experiences, vicarious experiences, social persuasion, and emotional states. These sources are integral to my H.O.P.E. system.

Habits connect strongly with mastery experiences because habits involve consistent actions that lead to small, repeated successes. When you form a habit, like practicing a skill every day or working toward a goal regularly, you build up a track record of achievements. Simply put, good habits turn progress into a series of wins, which boosts your self-efficacy.

An optimistic outlook helps you see the possibilities in situations, which makes it easier to be inspired by others' successes (vicarious experiences) and to interpret feedback positively (social persuasion). When you're optimistic, you focus on the potential for success rather than the risks or failures. This mindset helps you learn from others' achievements, believing you too can achieve similar things. It also helps you accept encouragement from others without doubting it, seeing feedback as helpful rather than critical. In short, optimism makes you more open to seeing the good in others' experiences and supportive words, reinforcing your own belief in your abilities (Bandura, 1999).

Incorporating purpose, passion, and perseverance into your life strengthens all four sources of self-efficacy, ultimately helping you overcome challenges, improve your skills, and boost your belief in your ability to succeed. Purpose provides direction and motivation, enhancing mastery experiences, vicarious experiences, social persuasion, and emotional resilience. Passion fuels perseverance and engagement, leading to more frequent mastery experiences, stronger vicarious experiences, and heightened social persuasion, while fostering positive emotional states. Perseverance directly builds mastery experiences through sustained effort, encourages vicarious experiences by inspiring others, invites social persuasion through admiration, and strengthens physiological and emotional states by creating emotional resilience (Bandura, 1999).

Excellence connects with Bandura's four sources of self-efficacy because striving for excellence pushes you to grow and face challenges in a way that builds confidence and belief in your abilities. Pursuing excellence involves putting in the effort to improve and succeed, which leads to repeated success. These successes build your confidence and competence, reinforcing your belief that you can achieve difficult goals. When you aim for excellence, you often look up to others who have achieved great things. Seeing their success shows you excellence is possible, and it inspires you to believe you can achieve it too. Excellence often attracts feedback from others – whether it's praise, encouragement, or constructive criticism. Positive feedback from others boosts your belief in your abilities, making it easier to keep pushing forward. Striving for excellence can help you manage emotions like stress or anxiety, especially as you face challenges. In time, you learn how to stay calm and focused, which strengthens your emotional resilience and helps you stay confident, even when things get tough. In short, excellence leads to progress in all four areas, making it a powerful driver of self-efficacy (Bandura, 1997).

Building on the importance of self-efficacy and the factors that influence it, I strongly believe in social emotional learning (SEL). SEL is the footing on which all learning and growth occurs. CASEL provides a framework of core competencies for social emotional learning (CASEL, March 2023). The core competencies include self-awareness, self-management, responsible decision-making, relationship skills, and social-awareness. Each of these components are essential in developing a basis for all learning. For this reason, I will begin each chapter with self-reflection: a personal, sometimes vulnerable, story that has helped me develop self-efficacy and leader efficacy and has shaped my H.O.P.E system. Self-reflection is key in becoming more self-aware. It is through consistent, intentional self-reflection that we learn more about ourselves, others, and grow over time. Through self-reflection, I've learned more about myself, my strengths, and my areas for improvement. This ongoing process of self-awareness is not only vital for personal development but essential for effective leadership and supporting others.

To build leader efficacy and collective teacher efficacy, we must first have self-efficacy. Collective Teacher Efficacy refers to the shared belief among teachers in their ability to positively influence student outcomes (Donohoo, 2016). In his book, *Visible Learning,* John Hattie identifies it as one of the most significant factors in improving student success (Hattie, 2009). With an effect size of d = 1.57, collective teacher efficacy is strongly linked to student achievement. In Hattie's 2023 publication, *Visible Learning: The Sequel: A Synthesis of Over 2,100 Meta-Analyses Relating to Achievement,* he reports that collective teacher efficacy continues to be a significant predictor of student achievement, with an effect size of 1.34 (Hattie, 2023). This effect size, though slightly lower than the previously cited 1.57, remains substantial and underscores the impact of teachers' collective beliefs in their ability to influence student outcomes. Collective teacher efficacy requires us to believe in our own ability to succeed, collaborate with others, and inspire those around us. By focusing on fostering self-efficacy, we can improve outcomes for students, educators, and the entire learning community.

In the upcoming chapters, I encourage you to use the information shared to reflect on and build your own self-awareness and self-efficacy through my H.O.P.E. system. Each of the next four chapters – Habits, Optimistic Outlook, Purpose, Passion, Perseverance, and Excellence – will delve into a key element of this system. As you explore these concepts, you will gain valuable tools and insights that will empower you to grow, reflect, and lead with greater purpose and impact.

CHAPTER TWO
H is for Habits

"In any given moment, we have two options: to step forward into growth or to step back into safety."
~Abraham Maslow

Leadership can often feel lonely – whether you're a teacher in the classroom, a principal in a school, or a superintendent in a district. However, leadership is also genuinely rewarding. In every classroom, building, and district, leaders are present at all levels. Everyone has leadership potential, and greatness lives within each of us.

To lead others well, we must first lead ourselves well. Most of us carry trauma or adversity with us; it is part of who we are, but it does not have to define who we become. That's why Maslow's quote is so powerful, "In any given moment, we have two options: to step forward into growth or to step back into safety." Becoming the leader you're meant to be is a process that begins with self-reflection. To build self-efficacy, we must intentionally reflect on our habits, identifying those that foster growth in our pursuit of becoming our best selves. This is how we improve self-awareness and build self-efficacy. This is how we lead with H.O.P.E.

SELF-REFLECTION

When I became the principal of Ramsey Grade School, I was both excited and terrified. This was the school where I had grown up, where my husband, children, and even my parents had attended. It felt like a dream come true but also like I had been handed an enormous responsibility. The weight of it all pressed heavily on me. I had so much to learn, and failure wasn't an option. It felt like too much was at stake – not just for me, but for my family, my community, and the students who were now looking to me for leadership.

At first, I found myself paralyzed by imposter syndrome. I questioned whether I truly belonged in this role. Every decision, no matter how small, felt like it was being scrutinized, and I couldn't shake the feeling I was faking it. The thoughts swirled in my mind: What if I fail? What if I let everyone down? What if I'm not cut out for this? I thought I was the only one experiencing these doubts, but eventually, I realized imposter syndrome is something many high-achieving people wrestle with. I was no exception. It had created a constant undercurrent of anxiety, undermining my confidence even though I was surrounded by people who believed in me.

It wasn't just a moment of fear; it was a season of struggle. Every day felt like an uphill battle. The stress built, and I started to withdraw, second-guessing myself at every turn. I avoided confrontation, hesitated to make decisions, and became consumed by the idea of making the wrong choice. But I had to keep showing up because it was the one thing I could control. Each day, no matter how scared or uncertain I felt, I forced myself to face the challenges head-on. And something remarkable happened. Slowly, I began to change. I started to realize growth doesn't happen when you stay in your comfort zone. It happens when you step into the discomfort, when you take risks, and when you learn to show up, even when the fear is overwhelming.

One afternoon, as I sat at my desk, reflecting on the days and weeks that had passed, I remembered a quote by Theodore Roosevelt I had read years ago. It profoundly affected me:

> "It is not the critic who counts; not the man who points out how the strong man stumbles, or where the doer of deeds could have done them better. The credit belongs to the man who is actually in the arena, whose face is marred by dust and sweat and blood… who at the best, knows in the end, the triumph of high achievement, and who at the worst, if he fails, at least fails while daring greatly…"

I thought about those words often in the following months. Leadership, as Roosevelt had described, wasn't about avoiding failure. It was about being in the arena, putting yourself out there, and striving for something bigger than yourself. And I realized the biggest obstacle I had faced wasn't the expectations from my community or the fear of failure – it was me, my own self-doubt.

The shift didn't happen overnight. But gradually, I started to embrace the process, not just the outcome. I learned self-reflection was not a one-time event but a daily practice. Through this practice, I began to understand my triggers, my strengths, and my true vision for leadership. And in doing so, I started to discover my own power. I learned to speak to myself with kindness, to celebrate my strengths instead of focusing on every mistake. I became my own biggest cheerleader, not my harshest critic.

Of course, I still have moments of self-doubt, but now I understand those moments don't define me. They don't have to determine the outcome of my leadership journey. Instead, I focus on the things I can control: my actions, my attitude, and my ability to show up each day.
With time, my confidence grew. As I developed self-awareness and built habits that supported my growth – empathy, gratitude, and connection with others – I saw a transformation not just in myself but in those around me. My leadership started to inspire those I worked with, and together we built a stronger, more supportive school culture. I wasn't just growing as a leader; I was helping others grow, too.

I began to understand the importance of building capacity, both within myself and within the people I led. To truly grow, I had to make intentional choices focused on long-term success, not just immediate fixes. Here's an example of what I mean: a small percentage of teachers consistently struggle with maintaining classroom discipline, leading to frequent disruptions and administrative interventions. By prioritizing targeted coaching, modeling effective strategies, and providing structured support, I helped teachers build stronger management skills, ultimately creating a more stable learning environment for all. By understanding the Pareto principle and respecting my margins, I learned how to prioritize effectively and avoid burnout. And most importantly, I learned leadership is not a destination but a journey – one requiring continuous learning, self-reflection, and resilience.

As I reflect back on those early days of uncertainty, I realize the most significant thing I learned was this: It's not about being perfect or having all the answers. It's about showing up, doing your best, and trusting growth will come, one step at a time. Even on the days when failure feels imminent, I now know it's okay to fail while daring greatly. Because in the end, it's not the critics who matter – it's those of us who are willing to stay in the arena, fighting for something bigger than ourselves. And that is where true leadership is born.

DEVELOPING SELF-AWARENESS

Self-Awareness is a process, and it is essential to personal and professional growth. I was in my 40s before I gained clarity regarding my purpose and passions in life and leadership. While I was a principal at McGaughey Elementary School, I had the opportunity to participate in the School Leaders Network through the Illinois Principals Association. During that time, I embarked on a journey of self-awareness, and I was introduced to the Enneagram.

The Enneagram test is a personality assessment that categorizes individuals into one of nine personality typologies. It can help individuals better understand their motivations, strengths and challenges. The Enneagram is often used for self-awareness, personal growth, and improving relationships by examining core values, fears, and behavioral patterns. The Enneagram offers a framework for self-awareness, personal growth, and improving relationships by examining core values, fears, and behavioral patterns. After taking the test, I gained a deeper understanding of myself, which led to significant personal growth. As a Type 3, "The Achiever," I am success-oriented and highly ambitious, always striving to meet my goals and make a positive impact. My core desire is to add value to the lives of others and be seen as worthy, while my greatest fear is being perceived as worthless or failing.

This self-awareness sparked by the Enneagram, required a period of reflection that helped me identify the underlying motivations driving my actions. I began to recognize patterns in my behavior, such as my tendency to push myself relentlessly in pursuit of success, sometimes at the expense of my own well-being. This realization prompted me to implement daily habits focused on balance and mindfulness. By incorporating self-reflection, setting clear intentions, and practicing gratitude into my routine, I created a framework that nurtured my growth and built my self-efficacy. These habits allowed me to recognize when I was driven by fear of failure and helped me focus on my strengths without becoming consumed by the need for external validation. Through consistent practice, I became more self-aware and, in turn, more confident in my ability to manage challenges and lead effectively. The Enneagram not only deepened my understanding of who I am, but it also provided the tools necessary to build a more resilient and effective version of myself as a leader.

I think it is important to add a disclaimer here. The Enneagram describes default settings. Others may call it your default success strategy. Every person has a default setting, but you have the power to change your setting. You always have a choice in whether you engage in any behavior, action, or habit. By becoming more self-aware, you will understand your behavior and make choices on how you live your life.

EXAMINING VALUES AND GROWING LEADERS

Habits are the cornerstone of the H.O.P.E. framework. We know, from a famous anonymous quote, that our thoughts become our words, our words become our actions, and our actions become our habits. It is imperative to establish habits that foster growth because they affect our character and, in turn, our futures.

The development of effective habits begins with a look inward. As school leaders, we must know ourselves – our purpose, values, and vision. The habit of self-reflection helps leaders grow themselves from the inside out so they can later grow others. This is how I learned that lesson.

I had finally achieved my long-time goal of becoming principal of the very school I had attended as a child. I had spent years preparing for this moment. After becoming a school social worker, I pursued advanced education with the singular goal of one day becoming the principal of my hometown school. Now in the role, I mistakenly assumed I needed to have all the answers. As challenges mounted, I questioned whether I was truly equipped to lead the school I loved so dearly. Yet my commitment to the mission never wavered.

In my early days as principal, I often focused outward – on problems to solve, people to support, and goals to achieve. But as I faced tough decisions, especially those directly impacting friends and family, I realized leadership required something deeper. Strong leadership requires a strong sense of self, so you can lead with clarity, resilience, and intention.

During my tenure as principal at Ramsey Grade School, I discovered alignment through the Franklin Covey's Leader in Me program. Its success stemmed from the shared values of the school community and our collective commitment to the program. The timeless principles introduced in this program emphasized values like fairness, integrity, honesty, and human dignity (Covey, 2013). These principles align with my personal beliefs and the values shared by many educators I've worked with over the years.

At a point, I realized self-reflection wasn't just a tool – it was a key habit. It was the groundwork for authentic leadership. By regularly examining my values, mindset, and actions, I became more grounded and intentional. My core values of faith, family, service and community became my compass. When I led from those values, I found clarity and strength. This habit of self-reflection not only made me a better leader but also empowered my staff and students to become leaders themselves.

HABITS FOR SHAPING SUCCESS

Over the years, I have developed inward- and outward-focused habits to positively impact performance. Some of those habits promote emotional regulation, decision-making, motivation, and focus. These intentional behaviors, or habits, must start with the individual but can then translate to the school, district, or organization. Below are habits that have helped me grow. I encourage you to reflect on them to determine which may be most beneficial for you and those you lead.

One of my key habits, which I've mentioned frequently in this chapter, is self-reflection. This involves critically evaluating thoughts, motives, and behaviors, which allow for course-correction and staying aligned with goals. I schedule time daily for setting an intention and self-reflection because, for me, what gets scheduled gets done. These practices provide clarity and intention for my life and my leadership.

Resilience is another vital habit built over time. Resilience allows us to bounce back from adversity and develop better problem-solving skills. My own resilience was tested when I lost my brother at age 15 and later when my mother passed away from cancer. My brother, Brandon, drowned on a rainy Saturday in May. He went into a creek and never came home. Divers recovered Brandon's body on Monday afternoon, forever changing our family. It was my first prom, and the very next day was Mother's Day. That weekend was one of the hardest of my life.

Yet, from this tragedy emerged goodness. Our community rallied around us, and our school showed incredible support. Brandon's classmates came together to create a memory book, a beautiful tribute filled with stories capturing his spirit. He was the class clown, a bit mischievous, but always had a heart of gold. His classmates, who now call themselves The 95ers, encapsulated his essence in that book, and I will always treasure it. Through adversity, I've learned to adapt, and resilience continues to help me face challenges.

Social connections, relationships, also play a crucial role. Humans need relationships to thrive, and building positive relationships fosters motivation, self-esteem, and success. One of my most significant influences was my mother, Nancy. She fought cancer with unwavering faith and taught me the values of character, perseverance, and compassion. Her life embodied the importance of service to others and left an indelible mark on my life.

Another pivotal figure was my high school English teacher - Mr. Kingery. Growing up in a household where neither parent finished high school, the idea of college felt distant. This teacher nurtured my love of learning, showed me the power of language, and opened the door to a world of possibilities. He made me believe I could achieve my dreams.

As a senior in high school, I had another teacher who, in her own way, inspired me to realize my potential. While Mr. Kingery encouraged me with positivity, this teacher took a different approach. She wasn't as positive and told me that if I didn't go to college right after high school, I would never go. Challenge accepted! Perhaps that's why I ended up in school for so many years, eventually earning my doctorate in educational leadership. Regardless of her approach, I am thankful for this teacher's challenge because it pushed me to achieve more than I ever thought possible.

I had many wonderful role models and have built meaningful connections and habits. Some of these habits, empathy, active listening, and gratitude, not only strengthen relationships but also improve self-awareness and leadership efficacy. Relationships are built one habit at a time, and it's these small, intentional efforts that create lasting bonds and personal growth.

Strong relationships require empathy, the ability to understand and share the feelings, thoughts, and perspectives of another person. From a school or district perspective, communication is often an area cited in schools for improvement. Active listening is an essential communication habit. We should listen more than we speak, using empathy to understand others' perspectives. Communication is not just about sending a message but ensuring it's received and understood. Finally, gratitude plays a powerful role in improving social connections by fostering positive emotions, strengthening bonds, and promoting a sense of mutual respect and appreciation. When you express gratitude, it builds trust and signals to others that you value them, creating a basis of understanding and emotional support. It also enhances empathy, deepens relationships, and encourages reciprocity, where acts of kindness and appreciation are returned. Practicing gratitude contributes to overall well-being, making individuals more emotionally available and open to others. In essence, social connections – whether with family members, colleagues, or friends – require the implementation of pivotal habits to foster meaningful, lasting relationships.

Incorporating these habits requires consistency, and they lead to personal and professional growth. As educators and leaders, self-awareness is crucial for effective leadership. When leaders are self-aware, they make better decisions, communicate more effectively, and create a positive environment. By cultivating these habits, we can lead ourselves and others to greater success. Through consistency and intentional practice, leaders can also build cultures of H.O.P.E.!

SELF-AWARENESS

Growth requires self-reflection and self-awareness, which are built on habits. Establishing routines aligned with your goals allows you to channel energy effectively and stay grounded, even when life feels overwhelming. It can be challenging to slow down and be intentional. Our days are filled with constant decision-making and demands. From the moment we wake up in the morning to the moment we lay our heads on the pillow at night, we are bombarded with information that requires us to make decisions and act. For this reason, creating space for reflection and connection is essential. Habits like stillness, mindfulness, and setting daily intentions provide the mental clarity needed to focus on what truly matters.

One transformational habit I made is the One Word Challenge. My husband, Jeremy, and I select a single word to guide our focus for the year. This practice promotes simplicity and clarity, helping us prioritize what truly matters and make intentional choices that align with our values. Over the years, we've embraced words like trust, hope, and joy, grounding each in a meaningful reference. While our faith often inspires our choices, your word could be anchored by a favorite quote, affirmation, or personal mantra that resonates with you.

Once again, I believe it's essential to consider the whole person – mind, body, and spirit – when forming habits. True and lasting success comes from balance. Focusing on only one aspect of life often leads to short-term progress but lacks long-term fulfillment. For example, habits that address only physical health might improve your fitness but leave emotional and spiritual needs unmet. Similarly, neglecting physical or mental health while pursuing spiritual growth can lead to imbalance. By acknowledging the interconnectedness of mind, body, and spirit, we can create habits that foster holistic growth and help us thrive.

The One Word Challenge is a powerful framework for fostering this balance. Choosing a single word encourages intentional habits that support your well-being across all dimensions. For instance, selecting a word like peace might inspire practices such as mindfulness, conflict resolution, or prioritizing rest – all of which nurture mind, body, and spirit simultaneously.

For the mind, habits promoting self-awareness, curiosity, and growth are essential. Reading, journaling, or reflecting on goals are all practices that build resilience and clarity. A word like trust could inspire mental habits like practicing gratitude or adopting a positive mindset – actions that strengthen emotional well-being.

For the body, habit formation often involves prioritizing physical health and vitality. Regular exercise, balanced nutrition, and sufficient sleep create the energy and stamina needed to pursue your goals. A word like joy might lead to physical activities, which spark happiness, such as dancing, hiking, or simply moving in ways that bring delight.

For the spirit, habits cultivating connection and purpose are key. Whether through meditation, acts of kindness, or meaningful conversations, these practices help ground us in our values and bring fulfillment. Words like hope or peace can inspire habits such as daily reflection, intentional stillness, or serving others – each fostering a deeper sense of purpose and connection.

The beauty of the One Word Challenge lies in its simplicity and adaptability. Your chosen word becomes a lens for viewing your decisions and habits, aligning them with your overall growth. This intentional focus creates habits that lead to lasting change.

Over the past four years, participating in the One Word Challenge has taught me the power of consistency. By establishing habits that align with your goals, you can create a purposeful and fulfilling life. Small, consistent actions compound, leading to meaningful and lasting change. What you focus on grows, so choose wisely, and let your habits guide you toward the life you want to build.

Regardless of your approach, habit formation builds the foundation for the person you aspire to become and helps you build capacity for yourself and those you lead. Considering the whole person ensures your habits not only support immediate success but also sustain long-term health and well-being. A balanced approach sharpens the mind, strengthens the body, and nurtures the spirit, empowering you to live and lead with H.O.P.E.

CHAPTER REFLECTION
- How can you integrate self-reflection into your routine?

- What habits can you develop to enhance your relationships?
- What adversity have you faced, and how do you build resilience?
- Reflect on your own communication: do you practice reflective listening? How do you ensure your message is consumed?
- Gratitude improves overall well-being. What are you thankful for? Be specific.

CHAPTER THREE
O is for Optimistic Outlook

"Optimism is the faith that leads to achievement. Nothing can be done without hope and confidence."
~Helen Keller

From the discipline of habits, we now turn to the power of perspective, exploring how an optimistic outlook can brighten the journey. An optimistic outlook, or mindset, has been shown to improve outcomes and produce better mental and physical health leading to improved well-being. Individuals with an optimistic outlook are more likely to exhibit a growth mindset, viewing challenges as opportunities for growth and improvement.

By fostering an optimistic outlook, individuals can enhance their self-efficacy, as they are more likely to approach challenges with resilience and confidence. Optimistic individuals tend to believe in their ability to overcome setbacks, which strengthens their sense of personal agency and motivation. This belief in one's capacity to succeed leads to greater persistence in the face of obstacles, ultimately driving growth and achievement. Helen Keller's quote sums it up, "Optimism is the faith that leads to achievement. Nothing can be done without hope and confidence." As these mindsets are nurtured, individuals experience improved well-being, stronger relationships, and greater success, contributing to a positive and supportive culture where everyone is empowered to reach their fullest potential (Fritz and Bicak, 2020).

SELF-REFLECTION

I grew up in a small, rural town as the oldest of three siblings. We were a typical midwestern family, grounded in routine. I believed I could take on anything. But one day in May, everything changed.

It wasn't just any day; I was getting ready for prom. I had picked out my dress, my hair was curled, and I was buzzing with excitement. I was 15, ready to celebrate the milestones of adolescence and the promise of what was to come. But in the blink of an eye, the world I knew was ripped apart. That afternoon, my younger brother Brandon drowned. My whole world came crashing down around me, and nothing could have prepared me for the depth of that loss.

In the following years, grief continued to weigh heavy. At 24, I lost my mom to cancer. Her illness was a brutal, unrelenting decline, and I watched her fade away despite every ounce of hope we tried to hold onto. And if that wasn't enough, my dad was diagnosed with Parkinson's and dementia, conditions which added a layer of complexity and heartache I never imagined I'd have to navigate.

I became the rock for my family, the oldest sibling who held everything together. But the pain, the grief, the responsibility was suffocating. And through it all, I merely survived. I kept moving forward, but I never truly healed. I didn't know how to heal.

Then one day, I was talking with my Aunt Patty. We were discussing my brother Dustin, who had witnessed Brandon's drowning when he was just 10 years old. Dustin had been through so much in his lifetime. I was telling Aunt Patty how much grief and trauma he had endured over the years. But she interrupted me, saying, "Well, you've overcome trauma too, Brandi."

Her words stopped me in my tracks. I had never thought of myself that way. It was like a light bulb flicked on. In that moment, I realized, despite the heartache, despite all the pain and loss I had endured, I had survived. I wasn't just the bystander in my own life; I was the one who had overcome it.

This was my "aha" moment – the point where I began to understand the trauma I had experienced had not just shaped me, but it had forged something stronger inside me. For the first time, I could see the resilience that had been there all along. I wasn't just surviving – I was surviving *with strength*, with purpose, and with a deeper understanding of who I was.

But thriving in the face of adversity doesn't come easily. It takes a shift in mindset. I realized optimism wasn't about ignoring the pain or pretending the grief didn't exist. It was about choosing to see beyond the darkness, about believing – even after everything I'd been through – there was still a way forward. Optimism became the lifeline I clung to in the storm.

I came to believe that life's hardest moments, those bumps in the road – the ones that tear us apart – are what we climb on. They become the very stepping stones to something greater, if we let them. But that doesn't mean it's easy. Every day, I choose to look at my grief, my fear, and my pain with the mindset that I can grow from them.

We all face challenges. No one escapes without experiencing some form of trauma. And when it comes, we have a choice. Will we allow it to break us, to make us bitter and stuck? Or will we use it to fuel us, to grow and become stronger?

For me, the answer is clear. I choose optimism, not because everything is perfect but because I believe in the possibility of moving forward, even when it's hard to see the way. I choose to thrive, not just survive.
That choice has changed everything. It's given me the strength to face life's challenges head-on, knowing I have the power to rise above them. And now, I'm asking you: Will you let life's challenges define you? Or will you use them to rise, to shape yourself into someone stronger, someone more compassionate, someone more alive than you ever thought possible?

The power to choose your outlook is life-changing. It's a shift from simply surviving to truly living. So, will you choose to see the light, even when it's hard to find? Will you rise?

POST-TRAUMATIC STRESS VS. POST-TRAUMATIC GROWTH

Maintaining an optimistic outlook despite adversity can be challenging, but it is a crucial skill to develop in order to lead a fulfilling life. It is easy to become overwhelmed by difficult circumstances and start to feel defeated, but focusing on the positives and maintaining a hopeful mindset can help you overcome those challenges. Finding meaning and purpose in challenging situations can provide a sense of control and direction. While trauma and adversity are inevitable, an optimistic outlook can help you navigate them with resilience and determination.

While watching television one day, I saw a segment on the news in which the anchor was interviewing an author about the release of their new book. *Under His Wings: How Faith on the Front Lines Has Protected American Troops,* by Emily Compagno, shares stories of veterans. In this news segment, they described the difference between post-traumatic stress and post-traumatic growth. It was an interesting concept; which caused me to dig a little deeper. Why do some people experience post-traumatic stress and others post-traumatic growth?

Post-Traumatic Stress (PTS) and Post-Traumatic Growth (PTG) represent two distinct responses to adversity, and optimism plays a pivotal role in determining which path an individual will choose. PTS is characterized by the lingering emotional and psychological impact of trauma, often leading to fear, avoidance, and a sense of being trapped by the past. In contrast, PTG occurs when individuals use their experiences of trauma as a catalyst for personal growth, finding deeper meaning, resilience, and purpose. Optimism is the lens through which this growth becomes possible – it shifts the narrative from *Why did this happen to me?* to *What can I learn from this?* An optimistic outlook doesn't deny the pain of trauma but focuses on the possibility of healing and transformation, empowering individuals to rebuild their lives stronger and more purposefully than before.

My brother, Dustin, has experienced post-traumatic stress. He has endured significant trauma throughout his life. Aside from being present when our brother drowned, a loss that acutely impacted him, Dustin witnessed death during his deployment in Iraq as part of Operation Iraqi Freedom while he was an Army National Guard Reservist. Though he rarely speaks about that period in his life, I know he experienced the devastating loss of fellow soldiers. Upon returning home, Dustin faced additional heartbreak with the passing of our beloved mother, compounding his grief. Post-traumatic stress is a part of his life. I believe, with time, we can all find a path to healing and peace.

I have also experienced trauma in my life, and I am constantly striving for post-traumatic growth. This leaves me wondering why. My only conclusion is we have to make a conscious choice to heal. We don't have a choice in what happens to us in this life, but we do get to choose how we heal from the trauma or adversity we experience. This knowledge empowers me, and I hope it will empower you too.

THE SCIENCE OF OPTIMISM

Optimism is a psychological trait associated with a positive outlook on life, and the brain plays an important role in shaping this trait. Studies have shown the prefrontal cortex, which is responsible for cognitive control and decision-making, plays a critical role in shaping optimism (Springer, 2021). The prefrontal cortex is more active in individuals who have a more optimistic outlook on life, suggesting this region of the brain may play a key role in shaping this trait. Understanding the brain's role in optimism has important implications for mental health and well-being. Optimism has been linked to a range of positive outcomes, including better physical health, improved cognitive functioning, and greater resilience in the face of adversity. By understanding how the brain shapes optimism, researchers may be able to develop new interventions and therapies to help individuals create a more positive outlook on life and improve their mental health and well-being (Psychology Today, 2024).

In 1998, my mom was diagnosed with stage four cancer and given just six months to live. The news was devastating, and she felt overwhelmed by hopelessness, even losing her will to fight. Then, she discovered a clinic in Mexico offering alternative cancer treatments, which gave her a renewed sense of hope. My dad accompanied her there, and my brother Dustin and I visited during her treatment. To our relief, we found her happy and full of optimism. She regained her purpose, dedicating each day to supporting other patients at the clinic. My mother shared her story and her faith with others being treated in the clinic. Her hope and positive mindset empowered her to live meaningfully, even in the face of her diagnosis.

After my mom and dad returned home, she visited the doctor who had given her the original diagnosis, but her prognosis had not improved. Once again, she wrestled with feelings of hopelessness, and her condition worsened rapidly. We were grateful to celebrate one final Christmas together before she passed away in January of 1999. This experience underscored the vital role of hope and optimism, shaping both my family's and my own outlook on life.

My mother's journey shows positive psychology, faith, and optimism can be powerful tools for overcoming adversity and embracing optimism. Positive psychology focuses on cultivating positive emotions, attitudes, and behaviors to promote well-being and happiness. Faith allows you to focus on something or someone greater than yourself. Optimism involves having a positive outlook and a belief things will work out for the best. Individuals who practice positive psychology, faith, and optimism are better equipped to cope with adversity and are more resilient in the face of challenges. Positive psychological interventions such as gratitude exercises and positive feedback reduce stress levels.

A study by Carver and colleagues (2005) found that breast cancer survivors who had a more optimistic outlook had a better quality of life and were more likely to engage in healthy behaviors, such as exercise and healthy eating. While it may not be possible to control the challenges and adversity we face in life, we can control our attitudes and behaviors in response to those challenges. By cultivating positive emotions and attitudes such as gratitude, hope, and optimism, we can develop greater resilience, overcome adversity with greater ease, and better cope with the challenges life may bring. I saw this first hand during my mom's battle with cancer.

CORE VALUES AFFECT MINDSET

This idea of cultivating a positive mindset is closely tied to the role of core values in shaping our attitudes and behaviors. Core values, the guiding principles in our lives, play a significant role in forming habits and fostering optimism, especially in the face of adversity. Just as I saw the power of optimism in my mom's battle with cancer, I've also witnessed how core values can influence one's perception of the world and shape their interactions with others. This brings us to the question: How do you view the world? For me, this question has often been answered through the experiences I've had with my students, particularly one named Raegan.

> *During my years working as a school social worker, I have fond memories of many of my students. One of these students is Raegan.*
>
> *I remember meeting Raegan after I had received a counseling referral from her principal. Raegan was a junior high student who lived with her grandmother. Despite being a bright student, Raegan's grades were slipping, and her teachers were concerned she had been experimenting with drugs and alcohol.*
>
> *When I went to visit Reagan for the first time, she was seated at her desk talking to her math teacher. Upon my arrival, the teacher exited the classroom leaving Raegan and me alone. I introduced myself, and Raegan quickly replied, "I have had several counselors; none of them have helped me, and you won't be any different." I simply replied, "I'm sorry about that Raegan, but I have been assigned as your counselor, so I will be coming to visit you once a week. How about we get to know each other a little better?" Reagan simply turned her desk away from me. So, I sat down and embraced the silence giving Raegan time to think.*

The next week, I returned to see Raegan. She sat in silence once again. I looked at her and gently said, "You may not have hope things will improve yet. Until you have hope, I will keep showing up and hold hope for you." Raegan didn't speak, but a small tear slipped down her cheek. Days turned into weeks, and I continued to visit Raegan weekly, providing counseling. I encouraged Raegan with simple acts of kindness and faith in her potential.

Over time, Raegan began to change. Her eyes no longer looked so far away, and her smile slowly returned. Over the years, Raegan continued to struggle in her relationships. She was self-medicating with drugs and alcohol. And later, she was placed in an alternative school and then, a residential home due to her behavior. Through all of those trials, I made sure Raegan knew I wanted to be part of her life. I was still holding hope for her for a better, more joyful life. I called to check in on her and visited Raegan when she was in the alternative school, the hospital, and the residential home. During one of our visits, we even went shopping. I loved that girl and wanted only the best for her.

I had a soft spot in my heart for Raegan, maybe because my daughter was only a few years younger than Raegan. Whatever the reason, I knew she needed someone to show up for her in this life. My purpose and values are what compelled me to keep showing up for Raegan. Through our time together, I knew her home life wasn't the best. Her mom was an addict, and Raegan missed something I'm not sure she ever had. Raegan desperately wanted a sense of belonging and family. That is what she valued.

So many years later, Raegan found what I think she was always looking for. She is married with three beautiful children. She has her own business, and she has a family. I am so proud of the woman she has become, and now, she has the capacity to hold hope not only for herself but for someone else too.

This journey of growth and transformation is deeply rooted in my own core values, which have always been faith, family, service, and community. My faith has always been my number one value driving my decisions. Next is my family. My life experiences have highlighted the importance of family. The importance of enjoying every moment with those I love, most likely because of the loss I experienced early in my life. Service has also been a cornerstone of my values, as I've learned the profound impact of helping others, whether through offering support during times of grief or volunteering in my community. Serving others not only strengthens bonds but also deepens our sense of purpose and connection to the world around us. Community is also one of my core values. This began when my brother drowned, and my school community supported our family by providing us with support through check-ins, a memory book created by Brandon's classmates, and by celebrating Brandon many years later at what would have been his high school graduation.

My core values have been incredibly important in helping me navigate life's journey. An individual's core values can have a significant impact on their mindset and attitude. By identifying and aligning with core values, individuals can develop a more positive and fulfilling approach to life, ultimately leading to greater well-being and happiness. Leading from your core values can improve outcomes for yourself and others.

SPREADING OPTIMIST THROUGH OUR STORY

Brené Brown says, "Owning our story and loving ourselves through that process is the bravest thing we will ever do" (Brown, 2010). We all have a story to tell, and sharing our story sparks hope and optimism by creating connections, fostering understanding, and highlighting resilience. When we share personal experiences, especially those of overcoming challenges, we remind others they are not alone in their struggles. Stories of perseverance can inspire others to see their own potential for growth and healing. They also shift focus from adversity to the possibility of triumph, or post-traumatic growth, igniting faith in brighter outcomes.

Here is a story of how my friend, Lisa Moreland – a teacher at Ramsey Grade School, has also overcome adversity in her life.

> *My husband and I got married when I was 30 and he was 38. Both of us were so used to living single, having a baby wasn't an immediate priority – getting used to married life came first. After a few years, we weren't getting any younger, so we started trying to conceive. I always assumed the process would go smoothly. But I was wrong.*
>
> *I lost three pregnancies within a year's time. These are the most painful experiences I have ever endured. I felt like a failure, like I was killing my babies because my body wouldn't work right. The mental and emotional anguish was something I had never felt before and never want to feel again.*
>
> *My doctor referred me to a fertility clinic for further testing since all our blood work came back with no helpful answers. Honestly, I wasn't sure a fertility clinic and in vitro fertilization (IVF) was our answer. I kept saying "If God wants me to have a baby, it will happen." But a friend told me, "Lisa, don't you think the scientific knowledge those doctors have came from God?" Hmmm… okay. Probably so.*
>
> *Our initial visit to the fertility clinic was for testing and blood work, looking for answers. I prayed and prayed before, during, and after this appointment, so nervous and so overwhelmed. We left our appointment that day and did some shopping. While shopping, I saw a shirt that said, "Something beautiful is on the horizon." To this day, I know without a doubt this was a message from God telling me to not give up. Whatever was going*

to happen was going to be beautiful, and we were moving in the right direction.

All the blood work and testing revealed a complicated medical reason I was losing my babies. And while there were medical ways around all of it, nothing was guaranteed. But we did have hope, so we proceeded with treatments. I lost two more babies during IVF. My husband and I were down to our final embryo, which made me wonder if this was really going to happen or not. Where was this beautiful horizon? Was that shirt truly a message from God?

I walked into my final implantation appointment with my final frozen embryo and I felt peace in my heart. I walked out that day not questioning what our next step would be. I was pregnant. All testing for the next few weeks came back healthy and good. I chose a nurse friend to help me with the IV I had to have every two weeks, and we made it the full pregnancy with a perfectly healthy and beautiful son,
Jaxon Lee.

I had to have a cesarean section, and as soon as I heard the doctor say, "Hey there, little fella," I burst into tears of pure joy. Without hope, I'm not sure I could've made it through those trials.

While Lisa's journey was filled with immense challenges, it also highlights the strength of hope and the power of perseverance. Her story not only speaks to the personal trials she faced but also serves as a reminder of how adversity can be overcome with the right mindset and support. In fact, there are various practices that can help foster optimism and hope, even in the face of trauma. These practices, like the ones Lisa embraced, can be transformative in building resilience and confidence for a brighter future.

While there are certainly obstacles in overcoming trauma and adversity, there are also practices that can foster optimism and hope including connections with supportive people in your life. Sharing your story of fortitude, growth and resilience not only helps others, but it also helps you build self-efficacy and confidence in a brighter future. Positive self-talk, or affirmations, have often been helpful to me. Finding a quote, scripture, or saying has grounded me and helped me stay focused on the outcome I would like to achieve. Engaging in random acts of kindness. Rather than focusing on self, focus on spreading kindness to others.

Researchers find spreading kindness has benefits for both the giver and the receiver. Acts of kindness increase the release of feel-good hormones like oxytocin, serotonin, and dopamine, which enhance mood and reduce stress. Kindness fosters stronger social connections, creating a sense of belonging and reducing loneliness. It also contributes to a ripple effect, where witnessing kindness inspires others to act compassionately, spreading positivity further. Engaging in kind acts enhances overall well-being and promotes optimism by reminding us of the good in humanity (Harvard Health Publishing, 2019). I want to challenge you to test out this theory. Find a way to spread some kindness today and every day.

SELF-AWARENESS

I've always believed in the transformative power of optimism, hope, and kindness in overcoming challenges. I've witnessed how these practices can foster personal growth – not just for me but for those around me as well. Looking back, I realize these principles have shaped my life in ways I couldn't have predicted.

Growing up, I was naturally an over thinker, constantly contemplating the "what ifs" of life, especially when faced with challenges. I had a strong desire to lead, but a fear of failure often held me back. Though I found success in many areas, something always felt missing. I wasn't progressing as quickly as I'd hoped, and I couldn't pinpoint why.

Then, a particular period in my life became a turning point. It was a time of heightened stress, and the pressure I felt was immense. I was juggling multiple responsibilities, and with each decision I made, the weight of uncertainty seemed to grow. I spent sleepless nights overanalyzing every move, afraid any misstep could lead to failure. It was overwhelming, but it was also a pivotal moment in my personal development.

One evening, after a particularly challenging day, I sat down with my husband, Jeremy. We talked through my struggles, and he reminded me of something I had forgotten: "You're here because you're capable. You've made it this far because you've consistently shown up and done the hard work." His words struck me. I had been so focused on the fears of failure I hadn't fully recognized the strength and resilience I'd already demonstrated. I realized I was capable and had the tools to navigate this difficult time.

This conversation was a revelation. It dawned on me I had been overlooking something crucial: self-awareness. I had been consumed by external worries and hadn't taken the time to reflect on how I could grow from within. From that moment forward, I committed myself to being more intentional about self-reflection and embracing optimism as a tool for transformation.

I began to see challenges differently. I understood life's obstacles weren't roadblocks but rather opportunities for growth. Optimism helped me view setbacks not as failures but as stepping stones that could propel me forward. This shift in mindset helped me approach each day with renewed hope, knowing every experience – whether positive or difficult – was a chance to learn and evolve.

During this time, I also learned the importance of managing stress and protecting my well-being. I identified my triggers, moments when I'd start to spiral into overthinking, and developed strategies to manage them. Techniques like meditation, thought-stopping, and positive affirmations became part of my routine. These practices allowed me to slow down, focus on the present, and approach challenges with clarity and confidence.

One of the most valuable lessons I learned was the importance of boundaries. While I genuinely care for others, I realized I needed to protect my own energy in order to show up as my best self. Setting healthy boundaries wasn't always easy, but it was essential for my personal growth and well-being. By focusing on what I could control and letting go of the things I couldn't, I was able to approach my responsibilities with greater balance and focus.

This period of growth transformed my perspective on leadership, as well as my approach to life. I realized true leadership is not just about making decisions or achieving success; it's about being authentic, empathetic, and self-aware. Through intentional self-reflection, I became more attuned to my emotions, triggers, and growth, which allowed me to lead with compassion and understanding.

Now, when I face challenges, I embrace them with optimism and confidence. Life may still present its hurdles, but I've learned to see them as opportunities to grow rather than obstacles to fear. This journey of self-discovery has not only helped me become a stronger, more authentic leader, but it has also allowed me to inspire others to embrace their own growth and resilience.

Through this experience, I've come to understand leadership is about fostering an environment of growth, both for myself and for those around me. By embracing optimism, practicing self-awareness, and maintaining hope in the face of adversity, I've been able to navigate difficult times with grace and resilience.

I challenge you to embrace the same mindset. Lead with optimism. Prioritize self-awareness. Create an environment where growth is celebrated, even during the toughest of times. When you do, you'll find the challenges you face become opportunities not just to grow yourself but to uplift and inspire others as well.

So, will you choose to lead with H.O.P.E.? Will you allow yourself to grow, overcome, and lift others as you rise? The power to transform your life and the lives of those around you is within your reach.

CHAPTER REFLECTION
- Are you experiencing post traumatic stress or post traumatic growth?
- What adversity have you faced in life? How has it shaped your mindset or outlook?
- How will you choose to heal? What is the future you see for yourself and those you lead?
- Name three of your core values. How do your values affect your mindset/outlook?

CHAPTER FOUR
P is for Purpose, Passion and Perseverance

*"Purpose is the reason for the journey.
Passion is the fire that lights the way."
~Anonymous*

Purpose, passion, and perseverance are powerful drivers of success. When we cultivate these qualities, we build self-efficacy, which contributes to a sense of fulfillment and well-being. A growth mindset is closely tied to increased perseverance, passion, and purpose. Those with a growth mindset tend to experience improved outcomes and more success in their personal and professional lives.

In this chapter, we'll explore how to connect with, fuel, and sustain your passion and develop perseverance to enhance your leadership skills. "Purpose is the reason for the journey. Passion is the fire that lights the way." This anonymous quote, resonates with me. Purpose + Passion + Perseverance sparks H.O.P.E.! The ultimate result is overall success.

SELF-REFLECTION

Purpose, passion, and perseverance are vital motivators in life's journey – especially when it feels like the road ahead is challenging. Jeremy and I married young. I was almost 18, and he was 19. Shortly after, we moved into an apartment in Ramsey, IL, and I found out I was pregnant with our first child, Morgan. When she was 10 or 11 months old, I began taking classes at Lakeland College and was accepted into the nursing program, only to discover I was pregnant again with our son, Ryan. After Ryan was born, I enrolled in Greenville College (now Greenville University) to continue my studies. But midway through my coursework, I received the heartbreaking news that my mom had cancer.

My mother, who had dropped out of high school, eventually returned to school and became a hairdresser, beloved by her clients. She was a perfectionist but also someone who put everyone's needs before her own. When I learned of her diagnosis, I took time off from school to care for her. She remarked, "I can't believe you would do this for me," but I didn't hesitate to help with daily activities she could no longer do. I washed and styled her hair, bathed her, and helped her with all of her daily needs. She was an extraordinary woman, and I miss her greatly.

After Mom passed away, my father remarried just over a year later. My mom and Rhonda, Dad's new wife, knew one another. Rhonda was a pastor, and my aunt and uncle attended her church. Dad and Rhonda's marriage brought together two families, each with its own history and dynamics, which has presented a variety of challenges over the years. These challenges, many of which I could've done without, have provided me with the grit I need to navigate through tough situations.

I share my background to explain that these experiences have shaped who I am today. My story has shaped me into the person and leader I am becoming. Our backgrounds and experiences serve to strengthen our belief in living with purpose, passion, and perseverance. These lessons have not only shaped my journey but also highlighted the importance of staying grounded in purpose. As we move forward, it's essential to recognize how connecting with your purpose can provide the clarity and strength needed to persevere as we navigate life's challenges.

CONNECT WITH YOUR PURPOSE

Your purpose provides direction and motivation, especially when times get tough. Losing sight of your purpose can lead to burnout and a lack of focus. By reflecting on your personal values and mission, you can reignite your passion and re-align your actions with your goals.

As a leader, it's essential to stay connected to your purpose consistently. A helpful practice for leaders is to examine how their personal values, vision, and mission align with the organization's values, vision and mission. Revisit the reasons you chose to lead and how your motivations have evolved. This process of self-reflection, guided by the H.O.P.E system, can clarify your priorities and guide your decisions.

Engaging in meaningful conversations with your team members, especially individuals whose counsel you value, is another way to stay connected to your purpose. Seek timely feedback from those you lead about your leadership style, and explore ways to better support their needs. Listening to their perspectives helps you understand your impact and better align your actions with both your purpose and the organization's mission.

My purpose was born out of personal tragedy. After my brother died, I felt hopeless, but I was surrounded by love from a very caring school community. My purpose was shaped during that tragedy, and I will always strive to serve others and build community as long as I am able to do so.

Early in my career as a school social worker, I was given opportunities to support others through loss. I remember a student at Effingham High School who died in a car accident. The school community was devastated, and counselors were brought in to support grieving students. We provided a safe space for them to grieve and express themselves. In many ways, my role was healing for both the students and myself. Through these experiences, I've learned serving others, especially in times of grief, is deeply connected to my purpose.

Purpose isn't just about personal fulfillment; it's about having a reason for showing up every day. Many educators say their purpose is the students, but it's important to dig deeper: Why do you want to lead? Where are you leading? The answers to these questions will give you the vision for your leadership, and people will follow someone who is driven by purpose and passion.

FUEL YOUR PASSION AND SPARK H.O.P.E.

Once you're connected to your purpose, you must fuel that purpose with passion. Passion is the energy driving you to keep going, especially when faced with obstacles. Effective leadership requires ongoing, consistent, and intentional practice. Through continuous growth and self-awareness, leaders maintain focus and evolve in ways that inspire others.

Research shows that a leader's belief in their ability to influence and positively impact their team – what we call leader efficacy – has a profound impact on their effectiveness. Leaders with high efficacy are more likely to make decisions that motivate and inspire others. When a leader has confidence in their abilities, it creates a ripple effect of growth and achievement within their organization (Dewitt, 2022).

To build this self-efficacy, leaders must reflect on their past experiences, challenge limiting beliefs, and replace self-doubt with a narrative of hope and possibility (Bandura,1997, 1999). Leading through your purpose and passion allows you to spark hope in others by showing them what's possible. By cultivating this mindset of hope and possibility, leaders can inspire others to embrace their own potential, just as I saw firsthand in the story of one of my students, Addison.

> *Addison was one of my students when I was a junior high principal. She was bright, curious, and had a heart of gold. Addison was kind, compassionate, and always willing to help others, but if you made her mad… watch out! Her temper was legendary.*

> *School was always a struggle for Addison. It didn't come easily, and she'd faced challenges in the classroom for as long as she could remember. If you looked up "spunk" in the dictionary, you'd find Addison's picture – or at least, you should. The word means "courage and determination," and Addison was the embodiment of those words. Despite her spunk, she lacked a sense of purpose.*

> *By the time she reached junior high, Addison knew everything she couldn't do or didn't enjoy. What she didn't know was what she excelled at, what brought her joy, or where she fit in the world. I tend to be drawn to students like Addison. Some of my friends call me a bleeding heart for kids who struggle, but I believe they need an advocate and a guide to help them discover their strengths*

and sense of purpose. I'm honored to play even a small part in that process.

Before the end of Addison's eighth grade year, Addison, her mother, and I decided to try a different approach. Addison transferred to an alternative school, where she thrived. She made friends, excelled in her classes, and found a place where she truly belonged. More importantly, she discovered her sense of purpose.

That experience helped Addison realize life's challenges aren't obstacles to avoid but opportunities to grow. Sometimes, growth requires a change in environment, finding your people or your tribe. When someone doesn't thrive in one setting, shifting to a different environment can create the conditions for success. Addison discovered with purpose, passion, and perseverance, she could overcome almost anything. Her grit and determination continue to shine, and her greatness is undeniable.

Purpose, passion, and perseverance are the driving forces behind H.O.P.E. When we have a clear purpose, it ignites our passion and fuels our perseverance, even in the face of adversity. These three elements create a powerful synergy, helping us push forward with a sense of direction and the belief we can overcome obstacles. Purpose gives us a reason to keep going, passion provides the energy to pursue our purpose, and perseverance ensures we don't give up when challenges arise. Together, they form the base for hope – an unwavering belief things can and will get better.

This brings us to the concept of grit, which is a crucial element connected with the trio of purpose, passion, and perseverance. As defined by psychologist Angela Duckworth (2007), grit is the combination of passion and perseverance toward long-term goals. It's a vital trait for success because it helps individuals stay focused, motivated, and resilient in the face of challenges.

I think of my Aunt Sharon when I think of grit. Diagnosed with cancer of the tongue, she has undergone numerous treatments and surgeries, yet she continues to live her life with determination, love, and support for her family. At over 80 years old, she still attends her grandchildren's sporting events and checks in on her siblings. Aunt Sharon's unwavering commitment to her family is a powerful example of love and grit. We should all be blessed with an Aunt Sharon.

SELF-AWARENESS

Aunt Sharon's unwavering determination and resilience exemplify the power of grit, but it's through self-awareness that we truly understand the core of our motivations and the values that drive us. In my journey, I've come to realize the importance of self-awareness through executive coaching. Through reflective practices and seeking feedback from others, I've grown as a leader. I've learned that taking time to understand my values and priorities helps me stay aligned with my purpose and passion.

During the pandemic my world really opened up. I did not realize the numerous ways educational leaders could expand their professional learning networks. Throughout the pandemic, I worked at home and at school. As many people did, I had a hard time shutting work off at this time. I didn't always feel productive in my work. Then, I started joining live, online workshops, trainings, and networks (like Teach Better). It was during that time I learned about coaching.

I was fortunate to work in a district where the superintendent and board valued this type of support and agreed to pay for my executive coaching. We met monthly in a small group. Reflected on our practices, values, vision, mission and priorities. It was an intriguing experience because I was joined by administrators in other states. Hearing their stories helped me understand that we all face the same types of struggles in this work. Today, I still have a coach. He is always in my corner. He is my cheerleader when I am my critic. He tells me the truth even when I don't want to hear it. He helps me see my blindspots and redirects me to my purpose. I value his feedback and express my gratitude for the time and energy he invests in me each month. Thank you, Tom Mahoney, for always being an encouragement, a voice of reason, and one of my biggest supporters. Now, I am embarking on the coaching journey as well. I am giving back to leaders by serving as their encouragement, their coach. I hope I can serve others as well as my coaches have served me.

Leaders who fuel their purpose with passion burn bright rather than burning out. I also believe many leaders see their profession as more of a calling than a career. For this reason, tap into the habit of self-reflection, the science of optimism, and figure out what fuels your passion. What lights you up? Spark hope in your leadership journey, and lead with H.O.P.E.

CHAPTER REFLECTION

- What are the core values guiding your decisions and actions in life?
- How do you typically respond to challenges, and what can you learn from those responses?
- When have you felt most aligned with your purpose, and what factors contributed to that alignment?
- How do your strengths and weaknesses influence your leadership and personal growth?
- In what areas of your life do you need to show more self-compassion and care for your well-being?
- How do you stay grounded in your passion when life gets tough, and what tools help you maintain that focus?
- What feedback have you received from others, and how can you use it to grow and improve?

CHAPTER FIVE
E is for Excellence

"Continue to do common things in an uncommon way. Continue to be 'all in.' Continue to apply 'best is the standard.' Continue to be a person of excellence in everything you do."
~Dabo Swinney

Excellence is not just a singular moment of achievement, but the ongoing process of becoming our best selves every day. It is the sum of our actions, habits, and mindset – each playing a critical role in shaping who we are and who we become. As Dabo Swinney eloquently puts it, "Continue to do common things in an uncommon way. Continue to be 'all in.' Continue to apply 'best is the standard.' Continue to be a person of excellence in everything you do." This quote encapsulates the essence of what true excellence looks like. It's not about occasional bursts of effort, but about consistently showing up and putting in the work. Excellence is the core of daily actions, rooted in good habits, and driven by a mindset that pushes us to constantly grow and improve (Given, 2017).

When we pursue excellence, we are not only seeking to achieve a goal or complete a task but to elevate our entire approach to life. It becomes a guiding principle shaping every decision we make and every action we take. Excellence serves as a powerful vehicle for becoming the best version of ourselves – whether it's in our personal lives, careers, or relationships.

Excellence, in schools and organizations, doesn't happen in isolation. Two statements are true. People need people *and* hurting people hurt people. So, when this is true, how do we achieve excellence? The short answer is clarity.

As Brené Brown wisely states, "Clear is kind" (Brown, 2018). When expectations are clearly defined and consistently upheld, individuals are more likely to engage in responsible behavior, leading to better outcomes. When people understand what is expected of them and are held accountable, they become more motivated and committed to their goals. This accountability fosters improved performance in all areas of life. Excellence is a path, not a destination, and it requires consistent alignment of our actions, habits, and mindset so we can truly become the best version of who we are meant to be.

The same principle applies to everyone: students, staff, and leaders. When expectations for excellence are clearly communicated and enforced, positive relationships are strengthened. By incorporating clear expectations and accountability into our systems, we create an environment where success is more achievable for everyone.

What excellence looks like can vary from person to person. The key to growth lies in the process, steadily getting better each day. It's not about competing with others but rather measuring progress based on your own continuous growth and improvement, consistently getting one percent better every day. As James Clear explains in *Atomic Habits*, small, consistent changes (1% better every day) compound over time, leading to remarkable transformation. By helping individuals understand the expectations and holding them accountable, we encourage a sense of responsibility and self-discipline. This leads to improved behavior, increased motivation, better performance, stronger relationships, and overall success.

SELF-REFLECTION

As the oldest of three children, I had a fair amount of responsibility. Each of my parents owned their own businesses and worked long hours. I babysat, cooked, cleaned, and was generally a responsible kid. I recall one day, my mother told me to mop the floor – I was about nine years old at the time. When I finished, my mom inspected it and decided I had not done a good enough job. So, she mopped the floor again. I didn't think much of this incident at the time and went into the living room and watched television. Years later, I remember these types of incidents from my childhood. My mom would often say "If you want something done right, you need to do it yourself." I respectfully disagree with this statement, but I have had to fight the urge to act on this mindset from time to time throughout my adult life.

In leadership, success isn't about doing everything ourselves; it's about building capacity in others and growing them to reach their full potential. To do this, we must clearly communicate expectations and provide constructive feedback. Feedback is essential to the learning process: helping others improve, develop, and gain confidence. While it may take more time upfront to build capacity in those around us, in the long run, it frees up time to focus on the work that fuels our purpose and passion.

Investing in others doesn't just involve directing them, it also involves investing in ourselves. Through self-reflection, I've been able to work through some of my blind spots. Instead of operating on autopilot, it's essential to take time to understand our own triggers and areas for growth. This self-awareness enables us to become the best version of ourselves and, in turn, be better equipped to lead others effectively. Developing self-efficacy in ourselves and others is the key to building lasting, impactful growth.

CREATING A STANDARD FOR EXCELLENCE

Creating a standard for excellence in your personal and professional life requires a commitment to highly effective habits, an outlook of optimism, purpose, passion, perseverance, and an expectation for excellence. By employing these practices,- you will gain a strong sense of individual self-efficacy – the belief in your ability to influence outcomes and overcome challenges. This confidence drives you to set ambitious goals, embrace obstacles as learning opportunities and persevere in the face of setbacks. With each success, your belief in your own capabilities strengthens, reinforcing a cycle of continuous growth and achievement. By maintaining this mindset, you not only elevate your own standards but also inspire those around you to strive for excellence.

Highly effective habits such as self-reflection, setting clear goals, maintaining a growth mindset, and prioritizing self-care, can help you stay focused on your goals and remain resilient in the face of challenges. An outlook of optimism can foster a sense of hope and possibility, which can help you overcome obstacles and stay motivated. Passion for your work and a sense of purpose can provide a deep sense of fulfillment and satisfaction. Finally, perseverance can help you stay committed to your goals and continue to pursue excellence, even in the face of setbacks.

An expectation for excellence can serve as a powerful motivator and ensure you are working toward a goal. When excellence is seen as the standard, everyone is encouraged to strive for their best and continuously improve. This can promote a culture of accountability and continuous improvement, which can ultimately lead to success for everyone.

> Sarah was a senior in the Macoupin County Creating Entrepreneurial Opportunities (CEO) program. She joined the programs with the goal of learning more about business, leadership, and personal development. The program was designed not just to teach entrepreneurial skills but to foster a mindset that would set students up for success in whatever path they chose to follow.
>
> Over the course of the school year, Sarah had learned a great deal. From mastering the art of communication to developing business acumen, each lesson had pushed her to become a more effective leader. However, it was not just the hard skills she had gained that made the difference; it was the soft skills that had reshaped her approach to life and to the future.
>
> The CEO program had introduced Sarah to the concept of highly effective habits – the cornerstone of any successful leader. The first lesson was about self-reflection. She had learned to embrace a growth mindset, believing her abilities and intelligence could be developed through dedication and hard work. It was a radical shift from the fixed mindset she had once held, where success seemed reserved for the naturally talented. Now, she understood perseverance and effort were the true drivers of growth.

In addition, Sarah had become more committed to self-care, recognizing that maintaining physical, mental, and emotional well-being was essential for long-term success. This balance wasn't easy, especially with the pressures of high school, dual-credit classes, and the CEO program, but learning to prioritize herself made her a more resilient leader.

Yet it wasn't just about habits and discipline. The CEO program had also helped Sarah create an outlook of optimism, an essential trait for leaders. Sarah was the type of person who worried about every possible outcome and often anticipated failure. But the exercises in the CEO program had helped her reframe her thinking. Instead of seeing setbacks as personal failures, she learned to view them as opportunities to learn and improve.

A sense of purpose had also begun to emerge in Sarah. She had always been ambitious, but her goals had lacked deeper meaning. Through her work in the CEO program, she had begun to understand the importance of aligning her ambitions with her values. Whether it was creating a business that helped her community or working to make her school a better place, Sarah realized success was not just about financial gain or status; it was about making a positive impact in the world around her.

The final lesson of the CEO program had been about perseverance. Sarah had experienced her fair share of obstacles, especially when trying to balance her schoolwork, personal life, and the demands of the program. There were times when she felt overwhelmed and ready to quit, but perseverance had taught her the road to success wasn't always easy. It was about pushing through the tough times and staying focused on the bigger picture.

Now, as she reflected on everything she had learned, Sarah understood excellence was not a destination but a continuous journey. It wasn't about being perfect but about striving to be better each day, learning from mistakes, and constantly improving.

The CEO program had transformed the way Sarah viewed the world. She knew the journey to excellence would not always be easy, but it would be worth it. And now, she was ready to take what she had learned and apply it not just to her future career but to every aspect of her life. Her work was just beginning. With the base she had built in the CEO program, Sarah was confident she could contribute to a culture of excellence – both at school and beyond.

Sarah's story is one of many from the CEO program, where students are taught success is not just about learning technical skills but about cultivating the right mindset, building strong relationships, and fostering a sense of purpose and perseverance. By creating a standard for excellence, they are not just preparing for careers; they are preparing to lead, inspire, and make a difference in the world around them.

THE ROLE OF SELF-CARE IN ACHIEVING EXCELLENCE

Rest isn't just about taking a break; it's a powerful tool for recharging, resetting, and framing the foundation for sustained growth. When we embrace the importance of rest, we unlock the potential to lead with H.O.P.E. Here's how rest to helps us achieve excellence in our personal and professional lives.

Excellence isn't just about doing more; it's about doing things well while consistently improving day after day. Excellence requires focus, clarity, and energy – resources that are depleted without proper rest. Whether you're an entrepreneur, a student, or a professional in any field, rest is essential for maximizing your performance. When we are well-rested, we can focus better, think more creatively, and make better decisions. Excellence is not about working longer hours, but about working smarter, and that includes incorporating rest as a crucial part of your strategy.

The most successful individuals and teams will be those who understand the importance of rest in resetting and thriving. Rest isn't just an indulgence; it's a key ingredient for building better habits, maintaining an optimistic outlook, staying connected to our purpose, fueling our passions, fostering perseverance, and striving for excellence. When we rest, we renew our energy, clear our minds, and strengthen our resilience. It's through this process of rejuvenation that we can continue to push forward with excellence. Rest is necessary to build upon the pillars of H.O.P.E., and only through embracing it can we hope to reset, recharge, and thrive.

So, take a deep breath, give yourself permission to rest, and let your H.O.P.E. flourish. After all, it's when we rest that we find the energy to truly live, lead, and make a difference.

SELF-AWARENESS

When I took the role of Superintendent of Mt. Olive School District, I was eager for the challenge. It reminded me so much of the district I grew up in – a small, rural community with caring educators and a close-knit, supportive atmosphere. I've always valued faith, family, service, and community, and I know from experience just how essential community is in a child's life, especially when that child is facing hardship or trauma.

There's a saying: "Every person is a lesson or a blessing." I didn't fully understand how true this would be in my new role. When you're in the middle of an experience, it's hard to see the lessons, but I believe it's important to stay grounded in your values. I've learned that to make a real impact, you have to align with the school or organization you're leading. It's about being the right fit and staying true to what matters most – your core beliefs.

My time at Mt. Olive taught me countless lessons. Some of the most profound lessons were about the importance of school culture – the way it shapes not only the students but the adults in the building. I've learned how vital it is to treat one another with respect, how to prioritize rest to maintain our energy, and how to strive for excellence without losing sight of balance. These lessons were tough, sometimes the hardest of my career, but they came with purpose. Through adversity and trials, there is growth and goodness.

As I've shared before, we always have a choice. We can choose kindness in our actions and words. We can choose to treat one another with respect and assume the best in others. Life's difficulties aren't always visible on the surface – everyone's fighting battles we may not even know about. So, be kind. Take care of yourself. Ask for help when you need it, and always build community. After all, as Helen Keller said, "Alone we can do so little; together we can do so much."

Now, it's time to spark excellence – starting with yourself. Reflect, build self-awareness, and believe in your ability to be excellent. The journey is worth it.

CHAPTER REFLECTION

1. How do your personal values align with the work you do? In what ways can you incorporate your core values into your daily actions or decisions?
2. Think about a challenging leadership experience you've had. What lesson(s) did you learn from that situation that you didn't recognize at the time?
3. How do you respond to adversity or hardship? What practices or mindset shifts could help you find growth and goodness in tough times?
4. What steps can you take to build stronger connections and foster community in your personal or professional life? How can you ensure you're being kind, supportive, and encouraging to others?

5. How often do you take time to reflect on your own actions and growth? What are some ways you can cultivate more self-awareness and self-efficacy in your life?
6. How do you balance your ambition with self-care? Are there areas where you might be overexerting yourself and neglecting your well-being?
7. Think about a time when teamwork made a significant difference in achieving a goal. How does the idea of "together we can do so much" apply to your own life and work?
8. What kind of culture do you want to create in your environment, whether it's at work, home, or school? How can you contribute to shaping a culture that values kindness, mutual respect, and excellence?
9. What does excellence look like to you? In what areas of your life can you start striving for continuous improvement, even if it's just 1% better each day?

CHAPTER SIX
Creating an Action Plan

*"If you fail to plan,
you pretty much plan to fail."
~Jillian Michaels*

Jillian Michaels says, "If you fail to plan, you pretty much plan to fail." With that in mind, it is time for you to dig in and build your own system of self-efficacy. Let's start by looking inward with self-reflection and self-awareness. As we do this, bear in mind any effective system should begin with clarity and intention – clear and specific goals and objectives that align with your priorities.

- **Identify priorities, strategies, and goals you want to implement:** *I need to be more of an instructional leader in my school.*
    - **Define what matters most to you:** *High quality teaching and learning are important to me right now.*
    - **Establish strategies that will help you stay committed:** *I will add time to my calendar, regularly check-in with my secretary for accountability, and utilize a visible scoreboard.*
    - **Clearly state a goal you are ready to implement:** *I want to regularly visit each classroom once every two weeks.*
- **Develop an implementation plan that outlines the steps, timelines, and resources needed to successfully implement your plan:** *In order to be a better instructional leader, I will meet with teachers to establish plans for supporting teaching and learning.*
    - **Outline the steps required to achieve your goal:** *I will schedule teacher meetings, and share an agenda to guide the discussion in advance.*
    - **Set realistic timelines and identify the resources needed:** *Meetings will last approximately one hour, and the agenda will cover questions such as current teaching strategies being used, areas where teachers feel they need support, ideas for improving student engagement and learning outcomes, and identification of professional development needs.*
    - **Provide a specific plan and timeline for execution:** *Following the meetings, I will analyze feedback, identify common areas for development (e.g., classroom management, tech integration), create individual/group plans and share with teachers.*

- **Regularly evaluate the effectiveness of your action plan and make adjustments as needed to ensure it continues to meet evolving needs:** *The school leadership team and I will begin executing support plans, including PD sessions, peer mentoring, and additional resources for teachers.*
  - **Regularly assess the effectiveness of your action plan:** *Follow up meetings will be held to discuss progress and challenges.*
  - **Identify what's working and what needs improvement:** *Discussions will be held collaboratively in PLC meetings to discuss what is working and areas for improvement with the goal of building self-efficacy and collective teacher efficacy.*
  - **Make necessary adjustments to ensure long-term success:** *Based on feedback, plans will be adjusted as needed to support teaching and learning.*

By taking these steps with intention and commitment, you are actively shaping a system that supports your growth and success. Now, let's get started!

SELF-REFLECTION

When it comes to self-reflection, establishing data norms is imperative to be sure you are making improvements, showing growth, and developing excellence. Over the years, I have learned data analysis is very important to progress and growth, and while some people thrive on data, I do not. However, I do love results and growth. What you measure is what grows. Measuring something shows you are prioritizing what is important. In order to effectively track progress and show growth, data norms must be established. Determine what you will measure, how you will measure it, and when you will measure it. Being intentional with data, data analysis, and how you communicate and celebrate results with your stakeholders is incredibly important to the growth process.

I created the H.O.P.E. Self-Efficacy Assessment to evaluate my system for building self-efficacy. This assessment uses the H.O.P.E. framework to provide an objective measure for progress. The assessment is designed to help you evaluate your self-efficacy across four key areas: Habits, Optimistic Outlook, Purpose, Passion, Perseverance, and Excellence. By rating the statements, which reflect your behaviors, mindset, and goals, you'll gain insight into your confidence and effectiveness in pursuing growth and overcoming challenges. Your total score, which ranges from 15 to 60, will indicate how strongly you demonstrate self-efficacy within the H.O.P.E. system. Higher scores reflect greater confidence in achieving success.

Download the assessment and following questions to build your H.O.P.E. system through the QR code.

H.O.P.E. SELF-EFFICACY ASSESSMENT

INSTRUCTIONS

Rate how true each of the following statements is for you using this scale:

- **1 = Not at all true**
- **2 = Hardly true**
- **3 = Moderately true**
- **4 = Exactly true**

HABITS

1. I consistently maintain routines that support my personal and professional growth.
2. I can rely on my habits to achieve goals, even in challenging circumstances.
3. I am able to adapt my habits when my priorities or circumstances change.

OPTIMISTIC OUTLOOK

4. I approach challenges with a belief that I will find a way to succeed.
5. I focus on positive outcomes rather than dwelling on potential failures.
6. I use setbacks as opportunities to learn and improve.

PURPOSE, PASSION, AND PERSEVERANCE

7. I have a clear sense of direction that motivates my actions.
8. I make decisions aligned with my core values and long-term goals.
9. I feel confident in my ability to pursue meaningful objectives.
10. I remain committed to my goals even when progress is slow or difficult.
11. I find ways to stay energized and motivated about the things I care about most.
12. I am confident in my ability to overcome obstacles in pursuit of my purpose/passions.

EXCELLENCE

13. I strive to consistently produce high-quality results in my work and personal life.
14. I set high standards for myself and take actionable steps to meet them.
15. I believe in my ability to achieve excellence, even in areas that challenge me.

SCORING

- **Add up your scores for all 15 items.**
- **Total Score Range: 15 to 60**
- **Higher scores indicate greater self-efficacy in the context of the H.O.P.E. framework.**

Based on your results, what areas would you like to focus on for growth? In the next section, we will start building a system of H.O.P.E. to support your goals for personal and/or professional growth.

IMPLEMENTING YOUR SYSTEM OF SELF-EFFICACY

Implementing a system of self-efficacy is an inside job. The first step is to engage in self-awareness through self-reflection. In the pages to follow, I will take you through my system in an effort to help you start creating an action plan for building your own system of self-efficacy. A system, structure or organized framework of self-efficacy can foster personal and professional growth.

First, we begin with Habits. Identify the habits you have already implemented in your life that have helped you achieve success, such as self-reflection, resilience, goal setting, or empathy. We must self-reflect in an effort to improve self-awareness.

HABITS: APPLYING PRACTICAL STRATEGIES

To move from understanding the importance of habits to actually implementing them, let's explore practical strategies for building habits broken down into manageable steps. For instance, instead of saying you want to exercise more, consider walking for 15 minutes every day. The smaller the habit, the easier it is to start. Simple, consistent actions build highly effective habits. And, consistency compounds. Track your habits, utilize (or build) a support network, and celebrate small wins during your journey.

REFLECT ON YOUR HABITS

Which habits are serving you well?

> Which habits can you use to build a system of self-efficacy?

> List the habits you have decided to start, stop, continue, and consider.
> Start:
> Stop:
> Continue:
> Consider:

> Be intentional. Write down the behaviors you should put into action to develop the habits identified above.

Habits are essential for creating consistency in both personal and professional growth. By establishing consistent routines, individuals create a stable base for progress and success. These habits help set clear expectations and create a sense of structure, which is especially important when navigating challenging or unpredictable circumstances. In both personal and professional settings, habits serve as the building blocks for continual improvement, enabling individuals to stay focused on their values and goals sparking success even when faced with obstacles.

OPTIMISTIC OUTLOOK: APPLYING PRACTICAL STRATEGIES

An optimistic outlook can be gained by reframing negative thoughts, practicing gratitude, cultivating positive relationships, and visualizing positive outcomes. Our thoughts are powerful and determine the choices we make and how we live our lives. In order to take charge of our thoughts, we first must become aware of common negative thoughts such as *I can't do this* or *This always happens to me*. In order to combat negative thoughts, it is important to look for evidence. What evidence supports my thinking or contradicts it? Then, reframe or replace those negative thoughts with realistic, positive affirmations. For example, *I can do hard things* or *This is challenging, but I can learn from it*. Reframing negative thinking is a powerful way to build an optimistic outlook.

Jon Gordon says, you can't be blessed and stressed at the same time. By starting your day with gratitude, you are starting your day feeling blessed. Write down three to five things you are grateful for every day. Build that practice into a daily routine. Express your gratitude to others and grow positive relationships in your life. Seek out individuals who inspire and uplift you. Limit exposure to the "Negative Nellies" in your life.

Visualize positive outcomes by seeing yourself successfully achieving your goals and overcoming challenges. When my son played basketball, I would often tell him to visualize the ball going into the basket. I got a few eye rolls over the years, but it works. A simple strategy for doing this is creating a vision board. Collect images and words that represent the future you desire, then visualize yourself attaining your goals.

By consistently engaging in these practices, we train our minds to naturally gravitate towards optimism. This evolved optimism, in turn, strengthens our perseverance, ignites our passion, and empowers us to pursue excellence with unwavering belief in our abilities. Ultimately, a robust optimistic outlook becomes the bedrock upon which we build a life of purpose and impact, leading with H.O.P.E.

Next, self-reflect and consider your outlook. An optimistic outlook is a reflection of who we are and what we believe in. Promoting an optimistic outlook can foster a growth mindset and a belief in their own abilities to succeed.

SELF-REFLECTION

What adversity/trauma have you faced in life?

How has adversity/trauma shaped your outlook?

How do your worldview, values, and beliefs affect your outlook?

An optimistic outlook is integral for personal and professional growth. Individuals who approach their work with positivity and optimism are more likely to stay motivated and resilient, even in the face of challenges. This mindset not only enhances your ability to overcome obstacles but also fuels your continuous improvement and commitment to goals. Ultimately, optimism strengthens the footing for ongoing growth and personal fulfillment.

PURPOSE, PASSION, AND PERSEVERANCE: APPLYING PRACTICAL STRATEGIES

Purpose, passion, and perseverance are essential in implementing a system of self-efficacy. As you develop grit and set priorities, you are able to achieve your goals. Stephen Covey calls priorities "big rocks." The big rocks represent your main priorities or long-term goals. "Little rocks" represent your day-to-day responsibilities and short-term goals.

"Sand" represents minor tasks or things that aren't important. "Water" represents the unimportant distractions that get in the way of your important work or main priorities. If you don't prioritize the big rocks first, you end up with a vessel full of sand and water. No matter how passionate you are, you cannot achieve your goals or accomplish your main priorities without purpose, passion, and perseverance.

Reflect on your values. Identify what truly matters to you and write down your core values and how they manifest in your life. Then, consider your passions: What activities make you lose track of time? What are the problems you feel compelled to solve? List your passions and consider how they contribute to the greater good. Develop a growth mindset. View challenges as opportunities for learning and growth. Build a support system and take care of yourself. Get enough sleep, eat healthy foods, and engage in regular exercise. It will not always be easy but it will help you develop a strong sense of purpose, ignite your passion, strengthen your perseverance, and lead with a greater sense of joy and fulfillment.

> **What is your purpose in life? Write down your core values and state how they manifest in your life.**

> **What are you passionate about in life? List your passions and consider how they contribute to a greater good.**

> **Do I model a growth mindset? What challenges have I faced, and how do I respond to them?**

Purpose, passion, and perseverance are essential components of a system that promotes success. When educators are passionate about their work and have a clear sense of purpose, they are more likely to stay engaged and motivated, driving both personal and professional growth. This sense of purpose allows individuals to stay focused on what truly matters, helping them remain committed to their goals despite the challenges they may face. Perseverance plays a critical role in overcoming these obstacles. Teachers and school staff who persist through difficult situations demonstrate resilience and determination, not only fostering their own growth but also inspiring others to do the same. By embracing perseverance, individuals can continue to push forward, stay dedicated to their goals, and evolve in their roles, ultimately enhancing both their personal development and professional fulfillment.

EXCELLENCE: APPLYING PRACTICAL STRATEGIES

Excellence isn't about perfection; it's about consistently striving for your best, continuously improving, and holding yourself to high standards. It's about a commitment to quality and a relentless pursuit of growth. Promoting excellence will raise the bar. You must know your expectations for excellence and be able to clearly articulate them to yourself and others.

> **Accountability - How do you define excellence?**

> **Clarity** - How do you clearly articulate your definition of excellence to those you lead?

> **Be Intentional** - How do you celebrate your accomplishments?

Excellence is essential for creating a culture of high expectations. When individuals hold themselves and others to high standards, they engender a mindset of continuous improvement and accountability. This drive for excellence creates a sense of urgency, motivating individuals to push beyond their limits and strive for higher achievements. By consistently aiming for excellence, educators not only elevate their own growth but also inspire those around them to pursue their best work, contributing to a culture of achievement and development. The pursuit of excellence fosters a culture of H.O.P.E.

CULTIVATING RESILIENCE THROUGH PURPOSE

Building a system of H.O.P.E. requires intentional habits and a mindset rooted in optimism, purpose, passion, perseverance, and excellence. Each element plays a vital role in creating a resilient and motivated community, whether it's in a classroom, organization, or any collaborative space. Habits, especially positive ones, are the ground upon which success is built, providing the consistency needed to push through challenges. An optimistic outlook fuels hope, reminding us setbacks are not permanent and growth is always possible. Passion drives our commitment, while purpose provides the deep motivation behind every effort, giving our actions meaning and direction.

Perseverance is the determination to keep going, even when obstacles arise, and excellence becomes the standard we strive for in all we do. Together, these elements create a powerful system that inspires individuals to continue moving forward, knowing that with the right mindset and habits, they can achieve their fullest potential.

Our purpose is what keeps us grounded and moving forward because it serves as our guiding light during times of uncertainty and challenge. When we understand our purpose, it provides clarity and direction, helping us navigate through life's obstacles with a sense of meaning and intent. Purpose connects our daily actions to a bigger picture, reminding us of what truly matters and why we do what we do. It anchors us during moments of doubt, motivating us to persevere when things get tough. Without a clear sense of purpose, we may feel lost or aimless, but when we are rooted in our purpose, we gain the resilience to continue forward with determination and focus. Ultimately, our purpose fuels our drive, it is our willpower, ensuring we don't just go through the motions but move with intention toward something greater.

SELF-AWARENESS

My system of H.O.P.E. has been in development for many years. I have spent over 20 years in education learning lessons, hearing stories, and living through trauma, pain, and joy. Everyone has a purpose in this life. My purpose is driven through my system of H.O.P.E. I am passionate about empowering others to grow, which is why I developed this system of self-efficacy. It has enabled me to spark hope in myself and others, helping us realize our fullest potential.

I am blessed to have served several school districts throughout my career thus far. I have met many wonderful people who have helped me become a better version of myself, and I believe I have helped them throughout the years as well. It was my intention to serve as a model, through my leadership, of my H.O.P.E. system.

We are all on a journey. We should always be learning, growing, and improving. This perpetual process of development helps us better understand ourselves and others and allows us to serve others well.

CHAPTER REFLECTION

1. What is your purpose in the journey you're currently on, and how does it influence your daily actions?
2. How do you define passion in your life, and in what ways does it fuel your pursuit of your goals?
3. Think of a time when perseverance helped you overcome a significant challenge. How did this experience shape your understanding of success?
4. How do you balance purpose, passion, and perseverance in your own life to maintain momentum toward your goals?
5. In what ways can you incorporate more intentional reflection on your purpose and passion into your daily routine?
6. What role does hope play in your ability to persist when faced with difficulties? How can you cultivate more hope in challenging times?
7. How do you measure success, and how do purpose, passion, and perseverance align with your personal definition of success?

CHAPTER SEVEN
Building a Culture of H.O.P.E.

"A positive culture is created when people feel safe to be themselves and encouraged to reach their potential."
~John Maxwell

At the heart of any successful improvement strategy lies the creation of a culture of H.O.P.E. – an environment where every individual, from educators to students, believes in their ability to grow, collaborate, and achieve excellence. This culture thrives when self-efficacy is nurtured and cultivated. When we create an environment that fosters self-efficacy, it empowers individuals to take ownership of their learning, overcome challenges, and realize their fullest potential. A community that believes in the power of growth and self-efficacy sets the framework for collective success and inspires everyone to reach higher.

As John Maxwell aptly said, "A positive culture is created when people feel safe to be themselves and encouraged to realize their potential." This idea is the root to creating an environment where everyone feels valued and supported in their journey of growth. A culture that allows individuals to be their authentic selves and encourages them to pursue their potential fosters the kind of atmosphere where both personal and collective success can flourish.

SELF-REFLECTION

As a superintendent, I've always known the decisions I make can have a lasting impact on the district and the students and staff we serve. What I didn't anticipate was how much those decisions would stir the opinions of others – especially those who, from behind their screens, seemed to always have something to say – keyboard warriors. Most districts have them, individuals who don't hesitate to voice their opinions on social media or through emails, frequently offering unsolicited feedback, criticisms, or suggestions. At first, it was easy to feel the weight of their words, to internalize their criticisms and let them affect my confidence and my sense of direction.

I'd be lying if I said their comments didn't hurt and sometimes make me question myself. In those early days, it was difficult not to let their voices echo in my mind, especially when their feedback felt harsh or unconstructive. I found myself spending late nights re-reading emails, overthinking decisions, and wondering if I was missing something. These voices – some of them loud, some of them subtle – had a way of taking up space in my thoughts, creating doubt and making it harder to trust my own instincts.

But then something shifted. One day, after reflecting on the weight of it all, I realized I had the power to choose which voices I allowed to influence me. Not all opinions were created equal. I began to understand I didn't have to listen to every criticism or accept every piece of advice at face value. I could take a step back and consider: Was this voice truly offering constructive feedback, or was it just noise? Was this comment coming from a place of genuine concern or was it rooted in misunderstanding or misinformation?

In that moment of self-reflection, I realized the power to choose what to listen to wasn't just a small thing – it was essential for growth. It was only when I started engaging in that power of choice, that I was able to step into the next level of leadership. The moment I took control of which voices I allowed to influence me, I felt freer. I felt empowered to make decisions that were aligned with my values and vision for the district, rather than making decisions out of fear of what others might think or say.

This wasn't about shutting out feedback altogether, it was about finding a balance. I still listened to the voices that came from a place of care and expertise, the voices of parents, staff, and community members who were genuinely invested in our schools. But I stopped giving energy to those voices that were quick to criticize without offering solutions or understanding. I realized sometimes, the loudest voices weren't the ones that mattered most. Instead, the quieter voices that came from thoughtful conversations or honest, face-to-face exchanges were the ones with real value.

And as I moved forward in my role, I began to see the difference. The more I exercised that power of choice, the more I grew, not just as a superintendent but as a person. I became more confident in my decisions, more resilient to criticism, and more attuned to the voices that truly mattered. I found true growth comes from within, and it starts with having the courage to trust yourself and make choices that align with your own values, rather than being swayed by every opinion along the way.

At first, it was challenging to ignore the critics. But with time and reflection, I realized every negative comment or unsolicited opinion wasn't a measure of my worth or leadership abilities. Instead, it became an opportunity to practice the power of choice – the choice of which voices to listen to and which to disregard. By making this choice, I stepped into a new level of growth, both as a leader and as a person. This lesson is one I carry with me every day.

BUILDING A SYSTEM OF H.O.P.E. FOR GROWTH

A system that incorporates habits, an optimistic outlook, purpose, passion, perseverance, and an expectation for excellence is essential for fostering self-efficacy and personal growth. By focusing on these elements, individuals can strengthen their belief in their own abilities and create a mindset that embraces challenges and strives for continuous improvement. Prioritizing these factors empowers educators to take ownership of their growth, build resilience, and sustain motivation in the face of adversity. When educators invest in their own development, they set themselves on a path to success and create an environment where they feel capable, confident, and driven to achieve their goals.

A LIFELONG JOURNEY OF GROWTH

For educators, growth is not a destination but a lifelong journey. The foundation of a culture of H.O.P.E. begins with educators, who must commit to their own personal and professional development. By embracing self-efficacy and a growth mindset, educators can navigate challenges with resilience and adaptability. This belief in their own potential to improve and succeed not only enhances their own practice but also empowers students to do the same. As educators model perseverance, self-efficacy, and a commitment to continuous improvement, they set an example for students, creating a dynamic and evolving learning environment where growth is celebrated.

When educators share their personal stories of perseverance and success, they provide powerful models of growth for their students and colleagues. These stories, like the ones shared in this book, remind us we are not alone in our challenges. They offer moments of vulnerability that help build connection and understanding, fostering a culture where both educators and students embrace struggles as opportunities for growth. In sharing their experiences, educators inspire others to reflect, heal, and gain strength for their own journeys. The act of storytelling helps create a deeper sense of belonging and solidarity within the school community and beyond.

BUILDING A CULTURE WHERE H.O.P.E. THRIVES

Ultimately, building a culture of H.O.P.E. in schools is not solely about academic achievement; it's about creating an environment where everyone feels empowered to grow, improve, and succeed. This culture of self-efficacy and hope helps students and educators alike develop the resilience and optimism needed to face challenges, overcome adversity, and achieve excellence.

According to Albert Bandura's work on social learning theory, sharing our stories is a powerful way to build self-efficacy and inspire others (Bandura, 1999). Bandura emphasized the importance of observational learning, where individuals can observe others' successes and struggles, and learn through those experiences (Bandura, 1999). Sharing our own stories allows us to provide concrete examples of perseverance, growth, and overcoming challenges. This not only strengthens our own sense of self-efficacy but also encourages others to believe in their ability to succeed, even when facing obstacles. When people hear stories of resilience, they begin to see possibilities for their own lives and recognize they, too, can navigate challenges and achieve their goals. Stories, in this context, become a form of modeling helping others visualize their potential and gain the confidence needed to pursue their own paths of growth and success. Stories have a remarkable power to remind us we are not alone. In a world that can often feel isolating, the act of sharing creates a sense of belonging. It's in these moments of vulnerability we realize many of us are walking through similar struggles, joys, and uncertainties – even if our individual circumstances vary. We all seek the comfort that comes with knowing others understand our fears, our hopes, and our dreams.

As educators, we have the ability to shape the future by fostering an environment where hope and self-efficacy are intertwined. This is what my friend, Lisa Moreland, did by sharing her story. Lisa's journey exemplifies the resilience and hope that drives the growth mindset. Her story, woven into the fabric of this culture of H.O.P.E., serves as a powerful reminder that hope can fuel success and perseverance can lead to the realization of dreams, no matter how long or challenging the road may be. By building a culture that encourages growth, collaboration, and a belief in our collective potential, we can ensure every student and educator is equipped to succeed, not just in the classroom but in life. This journey will require authenticity and vulnerability on your part. Are you ready?

We can continue to build this culture of H.O.P.E., one that inspires every individual to believe in their ability to grow, collaborate, and achieve excellence. Together, we can create an environment where self-efficacy fuels hope, hope fuels success, and our shared stories help us all see the path forward. Through authenticity and vulnerability, we create communities built on understanding, support, and shared humanity. And in doing so, we deepen the bonds that unite us all.

A crucial element of this culture is the power of sharing our stories. Our lives are woven with unique experiences, challenges, triumphs, and dreams that shape who we are. These personal narratives are not just reflections of the past; they are powerful tools for connection. When we share our stories, we open a door for understanding, empathy, and connection. We allow others to see themselves in us and, in turn, find pieces of themselves in others.

A CULTURE OF H.O.P.E. CREATED BY ALL

As a superintendent, one of my favorite moments of the day was walking through the hallways, usually before or after school when everything was calm and quiet. It was in these moments I noticed the full story our walls shared about our culture. Through the artwork on the walls, I heard the echoes of encouraging messages and felt the pulse of our past, present, and future. It was more than just decoration; it was a reflection of our culture.

A powerful new piece of art was added outside my office, and it left a lasting impression on me. It perfectly embodied our district's vision: Empower, Believe, Achieve. The mural was created during a community service day at Mt. Olive High School as a collaborative effort by our Art IV students and their teachers. Their work stands as a beautiful and vivid reminder of the culture that continues to be built at Mt. Olive CUSD #5.

As I reflected on this and other pieces of art throughout the buildings, I realized something profound: each piece told a unique story. These artworks were created by students and staff, all contributing to the culture of our school and district. It was not just about the finished pieces on the walls; it was about the ideas, the passion, and the collaboration that brought them to life. These are the values that shape the culture of the district.

SELF-AWARENESS

As I sat down to write this book, I had no idea how much it would change me. The process of putting words on paper forced me into a deep state of self-reflection. It was like opening a door to parts of myself I had tucked away, even forgotten about. The more I wrote, the more I discovered about my own growth and potential, and the more I realized how much power we all have to change our lives. Writing became a cathartic experience that helped me process emotions and experiences I hadn't fully dealt with before. It felt healing, almost as if I were taking back pieces of myself I had unknowingly lost.

In those quiet moments, I found myself thinking about self-efficacy and how vital it is for personal transformation. I had always known this concept intellectually, but it wasn't until I dug deep into my own experiences that I understood it on a higher level. The H.O.P.E. system of self-efficacy has the incredible power to unlock growth and potential in ways we often can't imagine. But it doesn't just happen. We must first be aware of ourselves – of our own strengths, weaknesses, fears, and aspirations.

Through this process of self-awareness, I realized something important: We all have a responsibility to not only recognize our own potential but to share that knowledge with others. If we keep our discoveries to ourselves, how can we hope to help others grow too? I realized I had something valuable to offer, a system that could fuel hope and success for others, just as it was doing for me. And though it made me anxious, I knew it was time to share it with the world.

This book became my way of not just telling others about H.O.P.E. but also holding myself accountable to it. I was vulnerable in sharing my own struggles, but I knew by doing so, I was modeling what it meant to embrace self-efficacy, to believe growth was possible no matter how hard life had been.

As I reflect on this journey, I now understand self-awareness isn't just about knowing what we're capable of – it's about knowing when to step forward and share what we've learned. It's about being brave enough to acknowledge our struggles and our growth, then offering that experience to others. By embracing our own potential, we invite others to do the same.

I invite you to reflect on your own journey. Reach out and share how you've used self-efficacy and the H.O.P.E. system to spark success in your own life. Your story matters, and together, we can create a ripple of growth, hope, and success that spreads far and wide.

CHAPTER REFLECTION

- In what ways do I nurture my own self-efficacy, and how can I help others develop the belief in their ability to overcome challenges and reach their fullest potential?
- How can I create space for sharing my story and encouraging others to share theirs in order to foster connection, empathy, and mutual growth within my community?
- How can I contribute to fostering a Culture of H.O.P.E. in my environment to help others believe in their ability to grow, collaborate, and achieve excellence?

CONCLUSION

"And now these three remain: faith, hope, and love. But the greatest of these is love."
~1 Corinthians 13:13

A system of self-efficacy is the keystone from which success is built. Can you imagine if we would have had a course on self-reflection, self-awareness, and self-efficacy years ago, maybe a course in high school or even college? The benefits, if you put in the work, are exponential for serving yourself and others well.

As I have said before, I was in my 40s before I felt I truly understood who I am, my triggers, my strengths, and my weaknesses. I understand I have not yet arrived, and I probably never will. Life is a journey, and if we are willing, we will learn something new each and every day. My system of self-efficacy, H.O.P.E. is such a powerful word and an even more powerful feeling, especially when put into action. Hope has the ability to help us overcome adversity, struggles, and tragedy.

When we turn on the television, there is stress, conflict and unrest. When we go to work, there is more stress. And, sometimes, when we come home there is even more stress. Everyone carries this differently, but we have a choice in the way that we treat one another. We must always remember, at the heart of everything meaningful is love. Love for yourself, love for others, and utilizing the power of love to overcome so we can lead with hope. "And now these three remain: faith, hope, and love. But the greatest of these is love." (1 Corinthians 13:13, New International Version). This belief strengthens my commitment to foster a culture of hope for myself and others.

Self-reflection has been a valuable tool for me in becoming more self-aware and achieving the goal of building a system of self-efficacy. My system of self-efficacy is serving me well as I strive to serve others well. It is my wish that you too will be able to develop a system of self-efficacy to lead yourself well.

As you continue this journey, I want you to carry with you a deep sense of purpose and empowerment. The H.O.P.E. system is not just a framework – it's a call to action. By embracing self-reflection and using the tools for growth, you'll unlock your true potential. Remember, you have the power to inspire, lead, and make a lasting impact. The world needs your leadership. Step into it with confidence and courage, and let hope guide you in everything you do – serve others, live with passion, and Lead with H.O.P.E.!

REFERENCES

Bandura, A. (1977). Self-efficacy: Toward a unifying theory of behavioral change. *Psychological Review, 84*(2), 191-215.

Bandura, A. (1997). *Self-efficacy: The exercise of control.* W. H. Freeman and Company.

Bandura, A. (1999). A social cognitive theory of personality. In L. Pervin & O. John (Ed.), Handbook of personality (2nd ed., pp. 154-196). Guilford Publications. (Reprinted in D. Cervone & Y. Shoda [Eds.], The coherence of personality. New York: Guilford Press.)

Brown, B. (2010). *The gifts of imperfection: Let go of who you think you're supposed to be and embrace who you are.* Hazelden Publishing.

Brown, B. (2018). *Dare to Lead: Brave Work. Tough Conversations. Whole Hearts.* Random House.

Carver, C. S., Smith, R. G., Antoni, M. H., Petronis, V. M., Weiss, S., & Derhagopian, R. P. (2005). Optimistic personality and psychosocial well-being during treatment predict psychosocial well-being among long-term survivors of breast cancer. *Health Psychology, 24*(5), 508–516. https://doi.org/10.1037/0278-6133.24.5.508

CASEL. *What is the Casel Framework?*. (2023, March 3). *https://casel.org/fundamentals-of-sel/what-is-the-casel-framework/*

Covey, S. R. (2013). *The 8th habit: From effectiveness to greatness.* Simon and *Schuster.*

Dewitt, P. (2022). *Collective leader efficacy: Strengthening instructional leadership teams.* Corwin.

Donohoo, J. (2016). *Collective efficacy: How educators' beliefs impact student learning.* Corwin Press

Draper, Kelly, Molina (2023). *Perception of School Leaders on Building and Sustaining Systems to Foster Collective Teacher Efficacy* (Doctoral dissertation, Saint Louis University).

Duckworth, A. L., Peterson, C., Matthews, M. D., & Kelly, D. R. (2007). Grit: Perseverance and passion for long-term goals. *Journal of Personality and* Social Psychology, 92(6), 1087–1101. https://doi.org/10.1037/0022-3514.92.6.1087

Fritz, S. M., & Bicak, C. (2020). Invited Essay Hope: Believing in a Brighter Future. Great Plains Research, 30(2), 109-112.

Gallup. (2019, October 22). *Engagement and hope positively influence student outcomes.* Gallup. https://www.gallup.com/education/267740/engagement-hope-positively-influence-student-outcomes.aspx

Given, M. (2017, October 17). *5 Leadership Secrets Shared by Clemson's Dabo Swinney During His White House Speech.* Inc. *https://www.inc.com/matt-given/5-leadership-secrets-shared-by-clemsons-dabo-swinney-during-his-white-house-spee.html*

Hattie, J. (2009). Visible learning for teachers. Routledge.

Hattie, J. (2023). *Visible learning: The sequel: A synthesis of over 2,100 meta-analyses relating to achievement.* Routledge.

Howard, Jacqueline. *Nearly 1 in 5 US Adults Have Been Diagnosed with Depression and the Prevalence Varies Dramatically by State, CDC Report Finds.*

Psychology Today. (2024). *Wired for positivity: How optimism shapes our well-being.* https://www.psychologytoday.com/us/blog/beyond-school-walls/202409/wired-for-positivity-how-optimism-shapes-our-well-being

Snyder, C. R. (1994). *The psychology of hope: You can get there from here.* Simon *and Schuster.*

Springer, A. (2021). *Neural mechanisms of optimism.* Springer. https://link.springer.com/article/10.3758/s13415-021-00931-8

ABOUT THE AUTHOR

Dr. Brandi Kelly is an accomplished author, speaker, podcaster, coach, and consultant with a passion for building thriving organizational culture. With over 20 years of experience, Dr. Kelly is dedicated to empowering leaders to inspire growth, create positive change, and cultivate environments where success thrives.

Dr. Kelly has received numerous accolades for her leadership, including the **NAESP Distinguished Elementary School Principal Award** and the **Middle School Principal of the Year Award**. She is also a Licensed Clinical Social Worker and a Maxwell Certified Coach. Recently, she was honored as a Marquis Who's Who Honored Listee, a testament to her impact in education and leadership. You can find her on most social media platforms and at sparkhopeedu.com.

BRING DR. KELLY TO YOUR EVENT

Are you looking for a dynamic speaker who can inspire and equip your community with transformative tools for success? Dr. Brandi Kelly offers a powerful and engaging presentation on the System of H.O.P.E., designed to empower individuals and organizations to create meaningful change. Through this innovative framework, Dr. Kelly helps participants unlock their potential, foster resilience, and build a foundation for long-term achievement. Whether for your school, conference, or community event, Dr. Kelly's message will leave a lasting impact and provide actionable insights that can drive positive transformation.

Let Dr. Kelly help your audience ignite their own path to success with the H.O.P.E. system!

Website: sparkhopeedu.com
Email: sparkhopeedu@gmail.com
Facebook: @https://www.facebook.com/LTW24
Instagram: @https://www.instagram.com/leadwithhope.23
LinkedIn: @https://www.linkedin.com/in/brandi-kelly-ed-d-lcsw/
Twitter: @https://x.com/jbmrkelly

MORE BOOKS FROM ROAD TO AWESOME

Taking the Leap: A Field Guide for Aspiring School Leaders by Robert F. Breyer

Transform: Techy Notes to Make Learning Sticky by Debbie Tannenbaum

Becoming Principal: A Leadership Journey & The Story of School Community by Dr. Jeff Prickett

Elevate Your Vibe: Action Planning with Purpose by Lisa Toebben

#OwnYourEpic: Leadership Lessons in Owning Your Voice and Your Story by Dr. Jay Dostal

The Design Thinking, Entrepreneurial, Visionary Planning Leader: A Practical guide for Thriving in Ambiguity by Dr. Michael Nagler

Becoming the Change: Five Essential Elements to Being Your Best Self by Dan Wolfe

inspired: moments that matter by Melissa Wright

Foundations of Instructional Coaching: Impact People, Improve Instruction, Increase Success by Ashley Hubner

Out of the Trenches: Stories of Resilient Educators by Dana Goodier

Principled Leader
by Bobby Pollicino

Road to Awesome: The Journey of a Leader
by Darrin Peppard

When Calling Parents Isn't Your Calling: A teacher's guide to communicating with all parents
by Crystal Frommert

Struggle to Strength: Finding the Ingredients to Your Secret Sauce
by Kip Shubert

Guiding Transformational Change in Education
by Kristina V. Mattis

Be the Cause: An Educator's Guide to EFFECTive Instruction
by Josh Korb

Called to Empower
by Coach Kurt Hines

The Blueprint: Survive and Thrive as a School Administrator
by Todd M. Bloomer

Sustaining Excellence: How Culture Drives Teacher Retention
by Martin Silverman

Culture First Classrooms: Leadership, Relationships, and Practices that Transform Schools
by Darrin Peppard and Katie Kinder

CHILDREN'S BOOKS FROM ROAD TO AWESOME

Road to Awesome A Journey for Kids
by Jillian DuBois and Darrin M. Peppard

Emersyn Blake and the Spotted Salamander
by Kim Collazo

Theodore Edward Makes a New Friend
by Alyssa Schmidt

I'm Autistic and I'm Awesome
by Derek Danziger

Emersyn Blake and the Stalked Jellyfish
by Kim Collazo

Birdie & Mipps
by Barbara Gruener

Teddy the Tiny Tree
by Derek Danziiger

roadtoawesome.net/books

www.ingramcontent.com/pod-product-compliance
Lightning Source LLC
Chambersburg PA
CBHW060838190426
43197CB00040B/2685